Project Queen

Project Queen © 2010 by Teresa D. Patterson

ISBN#: 9781470091750

PRINTED IN THE UNITED STATES OF AMERICA

Project Queen

A Novel

Teresa D. Patterson

CHAPTER ONE

S hae Byrts stepped outside to retrieve the newspaper. She just knew she'd read another headline about something happening on the south side of St. Petersburg. If it wasn't police brutality, then someone had shot or stabbed somebody else.

Things had just died down from the recent riots fueled when a white cop shot a black teenager and got off free. They had set the city on fire. Those crazy Negroes had actually burned up a news helicopter. The state ended up sending in the S.W.A.T. to calm things down. The racial tension could still be felt. The black youth of Saint Petersburg were consumed with an inner rage.

The ghetto-acting family in the apartment to the right of Shae stood out in the yard arguing. There had to be at least nine people living in a cramped two-bedroom apartment. So many people came in and out at all hours of the day and night. Somebody was always getting into an altercation. Last week it had been because somebody smoked up someone else's weed. Today, it was over the aunt sleeping with one of her niece's baby's daddy. Tomorrow, it would probably be over who drank all the red Kool-Aid or who ate all the collard greens.

The aunt vehemently denied that anything took place, but the other niece insisted she'd seen it with her own eyes.

"Auntie, you is lyin'," the girl yelled. The gold teeth she tried to pass off as a grill gleamed. "I saw Danny Boy comin' outta yo' room, zippin' up his pants." Her hair, braided in platinum colored plaits, hung down her back. They swung as she argued.

"You's a damn lie." The aunt rolled her neck and put her hands on her hips. "If you seent him, you musta been high or drunk." She looked her niece up and down while she moved her hand over her "waterfalls" hairdo. "And knowin' you, you was probably both."

"No, I wasn't. I mighta been a lil tipsy, but I still know what I saw." They pointed and got in each other's face.

"Auntie, you ain't nothin' but a hoe," the other girl said. "You don't be actin' like nobody's auntie. But dat's aiight. Danny Boy ain't no damn good anyway. You can have his ole limp dick ass. And I hope y'all used a condom 'cause I heard he gave his baby mama a STD."

"I ain't got to worry 'bout dat 'cause I told you I didn't mess with no damn Danny Boy. Now, y'all know me betta dan dat. I am not dat hard up for some dick. Come on now."

"You *is* dat hard up," Jookie Shorty shouted out. He was a known crack head who fixed old bicycles and sold them to feed his addiction. "You know ya ugly ass gotta sneak up on some dick and catch it. Ain't none comin' ya way voluntarily."

"What is you tryna say?" The aunt forgot about the disagreement with her niece and turned on Jookie Shorty.

"You heard me. Ya ass is ugly. Ain't nobody gonna sleep with ya ugly ass willingly. In dat aspect, I don't believe Danny Boy was ever in ya room."

"And how the hell do you know?" the niece that had started the argument asked. "Was you there?"

"Hell nah. I don't mess around with big ol' hambeasts like ya aunt. Hell nah, I wasn't there."

"Then shut ya damn mouth and stay outta our business."

"I get in whoever business I wanna get in. I'm Jookie Shorty," he said, pushing out his chest.

"Like somebody supposed to be scared. You ain't nobody Jookie Shorty, with ya broke, crack smokin' ass."

"You ain't nobody either. None of y'all," Jookie Shorty yelled. "Y'all just a bunch of food stamp bitches."

"Don't end up getting ya ass stomped by these food stamp bitches," the aunt threatened. All the women glared at him, itching to fight.

"Fuck all y'all," he said. "I been done went upside one of y'alls head with this monkey wrench," he mumbled to himself. Ignoring them, he went back to the bicycle he'd been working on.

Drama all the time. Shae was so used to it she didn't even bother to show any interest. Besides, one of the girls, Tia, couldn't stand her or her mama, Bertha. Bertha Byrts got into an altercation with her at a bar one Friday night. It was rumored Bertha cracked Tia across the head with a barstool. Even though Tia had clearly been beat, the drunken woman insisted upon taking the fight outside. Once outdoors, Bertha hit her with her high heel shoe and threw her into the bushes. Tia lost her wig and had to walk home looking tore up. It had been the talk of the projects for weeks.

Tia glanced at Shae and curled her lips. Shae did the same, showing that she wasn't the least bit concerned.

PROJECT QUEEN

Hoes love to hate, she thought. If Tia wanted a piece of her, she could bring her fat ass on. Just because Shae was cute, didn't mean anyone could disrespect her and get away with it. Shae had an attitude and a temper to match. She inherited them both from her mama. She wouldn't back down from anybody. The bitches of the projects knew not to mess with her if they didn't want to catch a beat down. She fought at the drop of a dime. She'd even fought some of the disrespectful boys when she was younger. The same ones were trying to get at her now. They still didn't know how to show respect, so she wasn't interested.

Project people made her sick. The projects made her sick. Shae hated everything about Jordan Park. The city had recently renovated the apartments, but in her opinion, it was still *ghetto.* No matter what they did, Jordan Park was located in the hood. Therefore, it attracted hood rats.

The majority of the women who lived in Jordan Park was younger than twenty-five and had at least one child. If they had more than one, they had different baby daddies. The baby daddies were locked up or didn't take care of their children. That left the women depending on the government for a check and food stamps. Jookie Shorty had been right in his assessment of the women: a bunch of food stamp bitches. He should have called them Section 8 bitches. A Section 8 voucher took care of their rent because they didn't work to earn a paycheck.

Usually, by the fifth of the month, most of the women would be sporting fancy hairstyles and acrylic nail tips. They'd show up at *The Galaxy* or *The Night Riders Van Club* wearing new outfits, trying to act all sadity. Maxi Mall and Cititrends would have made a major profit.

Shae didn't just think she was better than those women, she *knew* she was better. The only thing they had in common was their living situations. And she blamed that on her mama. She didn't pop out illegitimate children just so she could collect a government check each month. She didn't hang in hole-in-the-wall clubs, trying to catch some broke pimp's eye. Most of the men she knew, she tolerated them for one reason: they gave her money. She didn't spread her legs or lay on her back for one red cent because she had it like that. She wasn't a whore. But, if she had to be a whore, she'd never be a broke one.

"Damn Red," someone shouted, spotting her on the porch.

"What's up, Red?" came from another person.

"That's one hot piece of ass."

Laughter and snickers rang out. Tia and her family members rolled their eyes, but didn't say anything. Shae knew they just wanted what she had. Jealous cows. No way could their two hundred plus pound bodies compete with her hourglass figure. She was sexy and petite, while they stood there looking like the Pillsbury Dough Boy ready to pop out of their tight clothing.

Once, she'd overheard Tia bragging to someone about being a cheerleader in high school. She must have cheered for Hostess Cupcakes. Shae couldn't picture her big ass at the top of a human pyramid.

Shae smiled at all the men making fools out of themselves, trying to get her to acknowledge them. Not one of them had a chance in hell. She had to admit, she loved the attention, though.

PROJECT QUEEN

Just to get a wilder reaction from the crowd, she bent to scoop up the newspaper that lay in the yard. She made sure to turn just so- to give the guys a sneak-peek of the black, lacy underwear she wore under her revealing, mini-skirt. This gave the envious women who were watching her every move something to talk about. Shae didn't give a damn about them or their opinions. They could go tell the white people for all she cared.

She knew the men had been looking and that was her plan. She took her time straightening up. Then, her steps were slow and deliberate as she headed back toward the apartment. She paused to shake her long, thick, shoulder-length hair.

Shae was beautiful and she knew it. She'd discovered that at an early age. At eighteen, she'd filled out in all the right places. She possessed the body of a woman and it complemented her face. She had natural, fine, curly hair and hazel eyes, which added to her bi-racial beauty. She'd learned to use her looks to get anything she wanted. Her beauty would be her way out of her poverty-stricken lifestyle.

She knew it was only a matter of time before she made her escape from the hood. Her mother might be content to be poor; however, she refused to be stuck with nothing but rats and cockroaches for the rest of her life. Low-income housing would be a thing of the past. She just had to save up enough money to get a place of her own. *Somebody else's money.*

"I saw ya hot tail out there teasin'," her grandmother said as soon as Shae entered the apartment. "You gonna get ya self in a lot of trouble one of these days. Mark my words."

6

Her eighty-eight-year-old grandmother sat in a rocker by the window. She wore a colorful housedress and sported a stylish black wig with gray highlights. She rocked gingerly as she knitted an afghan to match the scarf she'd already made. She did it to pass the time, doubtful that either of her grandchildren would appreciate such things. They were too picky. They wanted to wear that garbage they saw the rap stars on TV wearing. Fubu or Hoodoo or whatnot. Well, she was going to finish it anyway.

She'd knitted every day since she'd moved in with them three months earlier. It had become a routine. Maybe one day somebody would appreciate her efforts. Knitting took time, and it was painful due to her arthritic hands. She wasn't going to stop, though. Not until her time on earth was up. She'd give up knitting when she gave up the ghost.

"Aw, Ma Violet, shut up," Shae said rudely. "You ain't got nothing better to do than sit in that raggedy chair and be nosey all day long. Stay out of my business."

"Fast behind lil heifer. You too hot at the mouth just like you hot between the legs. Gonna been done caught somethin' one of these days," Ma Violet huffed, paused her knitting, and glared at Shae.

"Just shut up, you old goat." Shae stomped into the kitchen. "You get on my last nerve."

"Watch how you talk to me, you high-yellow wench," Ma Violet warned. "Jus' plain disrespectful. You cuttin' ya blessings short and jus' don't know it. God don't like ugly."

"Whatever," she muttered under her breath, thinking that Ma Violet had been nothing but a pain in the ass since she'd moved in. She wished the old woman would hurry up and die or something.

Shae immediately felt guilty for thinking such thoughts. Ma Violet couldn't help being old. It wasn't her fault she'd fractured her hip and couldn't live on her own. She'd been forced to sell her home and move in with them. Shae knew Ma Violet hated depending on anyone for anything. Maybe that's why she stayed in such a sour mood. All she ever did was crochet and complain.

It hadn't always been like that. Years before, Ma Violet had been the best grandmother a child could ever want. When her parents would take them to visit, Ma Violet would always have a special treat, just for her. She'd either have a bag of root beer flavored candy or some delicious jellybeans. For some reason, Shae liked the black ones best.

Ma Violet used to keep large containers filled with potato chips on top of the bureau in her bedroom. Shae and Toby would sneak into her room while she was in the kitchen, open up the containers and grab a handful of barbeque and another filled with plain. They'd hide behind the couch and secretly eat them, giggling because they figured Ma Violet would never find out. By the time she had dinner on the table, neither would have much of an appetite.

They would never hurt Ma Violet's feelings by not eating her cooking, though. Instead, they'd take turns throwing most of it out the window where their dog, King, greedily gobbled it up. Ma Violet never knew the difference. If she'd ever caught them, she'd probably have gotten a switch off the tree and tore their legs up. She believed in the philosophy, "waste not, want not."

Shae's favorite memory of Ma Violet was of her being the flip lady. Shae would watch as she poured different flavored fruit juices into Styrofoam cups. Ma Violet would place them in the deep freezer so they'd harden. She would sell them for extra cash. Every summer, the neighborhood kids raced to Ma Violet's house with a pocket full of change. Ma Violet made the best pineapple flip in all of St. Petersburg.

Ma Violet's house had been filled with love and laughter. Everybody showed up on Thanksgiving and Christmas to celebrate family and togetherness.

On Thanksgiving Day, the smells of turkey, ham, pies, and cakes would have your mouth watering and your stomach grumbling. Everyone would gather around and join hands. Ma Violet would bless the food then everyone would dig in like there was no tomorrow.

After dinner, the women would clean up the kitchen and put all the leftovers away. The men would stand around sipping on eggnog laced with brandy or rum. Before everyone headed separate ways, the entire family would help to put up the Christmas decorations.

Shae could remember standing out in the front yard and watching the Christmas lights in the windows blink. It had become such a wonderful tradition.

Christmas had been a repeat of Thanksgiving with the exchanging of gifts included in the celebrations. Shae, Toby, and their oldest sister would receive so many toys they'd have to carry them home in a Hefty garbage bag.

Everything changed when their father left, and Mrs. Byrts began drinking. The visits to Ma Violet's house dwindled to once a month, and then quickly became nonexistent. They rarely heard from Ma Violet after moving to the projects. From time to time, she came over and tried to talk some sense into her daughter's head. Many times, after being severely beaten, her sister, Vivian, ran away and went to stay at Ma Violet's house. She hadn't seen her grandmother in years, though. It wasn't until her accident that Ma Violet reentered their lives.

Now, there she sat, rocking and giving Shae the evil eye.

"Shae, ya yellow ass ain't done nothing I done told you to do," her mother yelled from upstairs. She jumped and the past memories scattered and floated away like bubbles. "When you gonna wash these smelly ass clothes and change them pissy sheets on ya brothers' beds? You gonna have me get on ya ass, that's what you gonna have me do."

"Shit. You'd think I was a slave around here," Shae griped. She slammed some dirty dishes into the sink and turned on the water. "I hate washing dishes. I get tired of cleaning up all the time. But it's not like yo' big ass gonna do it."

"What the hell you did you say?" Her mother ambled down the stairs, her feet heavy on each step. She wore a deep frown as she glared at her daughter. "Mumbling to ya self gone get you hit in ya fucking mouth. Get ya ass up there and get busy."

Mrs. Byrts was a big, strong, no-nonsense type of woman. Her complexion was pale like her daughter's, and she had the same pretty face, hazel eyes, and naturally curly hair. Even though she weighed about a hundred pounds more than she should, her attractiveness still showed. If she wanted a man, she could pull one. She just saw no use for limp dick motherfuckers. All they'd ever left her with

10

was a wet spot on the mattress in the morning and a feeling of disappointment. She could have had a V8. She had enough trouble dealing with four hard-headed children. She didn't need to borrow more.

"Why I got to do everything?" Shae complained.

"Girl, don't start with me. This house better be clean when I get back from grocery shopping. Tell Toby to get his sorry ass up and clean out that refrigerator. If he can't go to school like he supposed to, then he can get out and get a fucking job. That go for you too, Miss Beauty Queen." Shae rolled her eyes. "You can stand there cutting ya fucking eyes all you want, but when I get back the shit better be done. You know you'll catch hell from my big ass if it ain't." She turned to Ma Violet. "Mama, you want something from the sto'?" She ignored Shae's huffing and puffing. "How 'bout some powdered donuts?"

"That'll be fine and some Maxwell House coffee, if it ain't too much trouble," Ma Violet said sweetly.

"Alright. I'll be back as soon as I can."

Shae sucked air through her teeth. "Right," she muttered. Mrs. Byrts threw her daughter a sour look, said nothing further then slammed out the front door.

"Clean up this damn yard," they heard as she made her way down the sidewalk.

Shae knew her mother wouldn't be back until some time after dark, if she made it home at all. Mrs. Byrts loved to frequent the High Hat Liquor Lounge. If she wasn't there then she was at Tom's Game Room or at the George Washington Bar. Lately, she'd been hanging out at Ike's Liquor Lounge #2.

She hung out, played pool, gambled, and got sloppy drunk almost every night. Shae couldn't remember the last time she'd seen her mother sober.

She had probably already started drinking earlier that morning. Shae knew she always kept a stash of bourbon or cognac on hand.

She shook her head in order to stop the thoughts. Drinking all the time couldn't be good for anybody. Plus, it was probably the reason her mother was always angry.

Shae turned to her grandmother, now oozing sweetness. "Ma Violet, will you wash the dishes for me?" she asked.

"Why should I? After all that sassin' you done? Nah, I don't think so."

"Grandma, please. I can't do everything she told me to do before she gets back," she complained.

"If you stop standin' there whinin', you could done started by now." Her grandmother had no sympathy for her.

"You old goat. I hope you swallow ya teeth."

"I hope you get ya hot tail beat and that's what's gonna happen if you don't do what ya mama told ya," Ma Violet replied. Shae rolled her eyes and her grandmother chuckled.

Ma Violet went back to her knitting. She glanced at Shae and thought, *What happened to that little, skinny, pigtail-wearing gal who had been so sweet? Just an angel, yes she was.* No one could tell her that her granddaughter wasn't the prettiest, smartest little girl in the world.

She remembered taking her granddaughter to a store called Dr's Pharmacy, back in the day. If anybody asked her, that store had outdone any Kash N Karry or Winn Dixie. It had been owned and run by black folk. Couldn't find too many establishments like that around anymore.

She took Shae there and bought her all types of candy and bows and whatnots for her hair. Occasionally, she purchased some of them jacks or a bolo bat so she and her little brother could have something to play with. She got tired of them climbing in her grapefruit and orange trees. She even caught them in the neighbor's mango tree. Those kids had been so rambunctious.

She smiled as she reminisced. The holidays had been the best. It had been family time and a reason to celebrate and feast on all types of foods. She loved to cook, especially during that season. Her favorites were collard greens, chitterlings, potato salad, dressing and sweet potato pie.

She usually started picking the greens the day before and would get started on the chitterlings because they took so long to clean. Boy, she loved her some chitterlings and hog maws. They didn't smell too good during the cleaning and cooking, but the finished product made her mouth water. She'd throw in a tad of baking soda and a top of lemon juice to take away the smell.

She'd cut up all her onions, celery, and bell peppers, too. Then she'd boil the eggs for the potato salad, make the corn bread for the homemade stuffing, and boil the sweet potatoes for the pies. The next morning, all she'd have to do was concentrate on the ham and the turkey. It had been such a great time of celebration.

How she missed those days. She'd cherished her family, always wanting to keep them close. It didn't matter to her that Jimmy B was a Hispanic. He'd been the one her daughter had chosen to marry, so she had accepted him wholeheartedly.

PROJECT QUEEN

When he'd run off and left her baby, she'd watched Bertha change. She started drinking that brown liquor, hanging in the streets, and whipping on her children.

Even though she believed in "-spare the rod, spoil the child,-" she didn't go for that. No matter what's going on inside you, you don't ever take anything out on your own flesh and blood. She'd tried to make Bertha understand that but, Bertha didn't want to hear nothing anybody had to say to her about raising her kids. Instead, she stopped coming around, stopped bringing the children. They stayed holed up in those god-forsaken projects not even calling to see if she was still alive. The shame of it all.

It had just about broken her heart. The only time she saw one of them kids was when the oldest one started running away. She tried to help, but from a distance. It hurt her to the core to hear about Vivian leaving home for good. She couldn't much blame her, though. If you kept kicking a dog, one day that dog was either going to get up and bite the hell out of you, or haul tail.

Bertha should have done right by that gal. Now, nobody knew where the child had gone. She hadn't heard from her in almost six years. Her heart truly ached from missing that baby. Vivian had run off to get away from the projects because she saw first hand what they did to her mother.

Now, here she was. She was in these dreadful projects right along with her evil-hearted daughter. She had to try so hard not to let her own heart turn to stone. It would serve no purpose to become bitter. If you focus too much on your own woes, how can you find time to think about helping anybody else?

The Bible says, *"count it all joy when ye fall into divers temptation."* She found herself still waiting for the joy to come. Maybe it would just sneak up on her suddenly.

Ma Violet sighed. She missed her house. Her home had been paid for. It had been safe, clean and quiet. She had peace there. She didn't worry about gunshots disturbing her sleep or drug addicts trying to break in. She didn't even have to listen to that loud rap music her grandson loved to play each morning. At those moments, she almost wished she'd been afflicted with a hearing problem.

Her home had been her pride and joy. Her husband built that house from the ground up. She raised four children there and had helped raise her grandbabies there, too. She sure did wish she could have kept it. She just hadn't been able to keep up with the maintenance of it after the accident.

But, it wasn't anybody's fault she'd slipped in the kitchen and fractured her hip. If she wanted to blame it on something, she could blame it on old age. God had His reasons. He'd sent her to live with her daughter to serve a purpose. She hadn't figured out just what that purpose was yet, but she'd wait patiently on the Lord. He'd let her know in due time.

Ma Violet put her knitting to the side and got up slowly from the rocker. She then grabbed her walker and eased onto it.

"I'll wash the dishes, child," she told Shae. "It'll give me somethin' to do besides look out that darn window. Ain't nothin' out there but dry grass and po', pitiful Negroes. What's wrong with the next-door neighbors? All they do is fuss and fight all the time. They got too many Negroes under the same roof, if you ask me. And what's the deal with the man wearin' all them clothes? Ain't he hot? It's near 'bout ninety degrees out yonder."

"He dresses like that all the time, no matter what temperature it is," Shae said. "They call him the Jacket Man."

"Well, he might need a straight jacket."

Shae laughed and felt the relief brought on because of it. Her nerves had been strung so tight lately because of her mom's constant hounding and complaining about everything. She didn't know how much more she could take.

Mrs. Byrts could be ruthless when she wanted to be. It was all about control. If they didn't do things her way, she'd make sure they regretted it. That usually came in the form of a firm, ass whipping. It didn't matter to Mrs. Byrts that Shae was grown and Toby was a six-foot-tall fourteen-year-old. It was her way or the highway.

"Thank you, Ma Violet," she said. "I'm going upstairs to get the twins' room cleaned up."

"Okay." Ma Violet watched her granddaughter run up the stairs. She could picture that little girl wearing pigtails once again and it brought her joy. Where had all the years gone? If it was one thing she could testify to, it was that God had been good to her. For more than eighty-eight years, she'd been truly blessed.

"Lord, I thank you," she shouted and made her way toward the kitchen.

Shae turned the knob on the first door she approached and cracked it open. She took a step back because of the smell. She held her nose, opening the door all the way.

"Whew." The strong, unwelcoming scent of urine assaulted her nostrils. Her six-year-old, twin brothers had wet their beds again. That made the second time in a week. She resented the extra work, but knew she had to do it because her mama sure wasn't going to. Shae had long since resigned herself to the fact that her mama looked on them as her personal servants. She still didn't like it, though.

Going over to the window, she threw them open, hoping the circulating air would help. She snatched the identical Spiderman sheets off the bunk beds and tossed them on the floor. She figured she'd just as well wash the pillows and pillowcases, too. Both boys slept curled around them and they smelled just as bad as the sheets.

Loud music interrupted the quietness of the morning, signaling her brother, Toby, had awakened. He always blasted his music, not having concern for anybody else in the house.

"Toby. Turn that shit down," she yelled, but the volume only increased. She grabbed the soiled items and took them to the laundry room. She threw them into the washing machine with some detergent. "Toby," she called again because the loud music was beginning to give her a headache. She slammed the lid on the washing machine closed and turned the knob to the correct setting. Once she heard the water running into the machine, she went to Toby's room.

Shae tried the knob but found the door locked. She knocked a few times but got no answer. Finally, she pounded on the door with her fist. She knew he heard her and it pissed her off he wasn't answering.

"What?" Toby opened the door so abruptly she stumbled into the bedroom and almost fell. His lips turned up in the corner. "That's what you get," he teased.

"Shut up."

"What the fuck you want? Why you knocking like you the po po?" Toby was tall and thin. At fourteen, he was still maturing. His seemed to be all arms and legs. "What it do?"

"Mama wants you to clean out the refrigerator," she said.

"So what?" He shrugged.

"So what, my ass. Clean it out, damn it. I'm not getting in trouble because of you."

"Get outta my face." He pointed his finger as he advanced toward her. His sister knew he was only playing. He towered above her, but she would bust his ass if he ever tried her. Shae had a vile temper when somebody set her off. He'd witnessed her beat down quite a number of people. She'd even had his back more than a few times. She didn't take shit off of anybody except for Mrs. Byrts, but only because their mama was slap crazy.

"Come on, Toby. Please," she pleaded.

"What I get out the deal?"

"You can hold any of my CDs for a week."

"Even the new ones?"

"Well, okay," she relented.

"Eminem?" he pressed.

"Yeah, that one too. I said *any* of them."

"I don't wanna hold CDs," he said. "I want money."

She put her palm up. "Whatever."

"I'm serious. You want me to clean out that refrigerator, you gonna have to pay me. Otherwise-" He pretended to chop her in the throat.

18

"How much?" she asked. She really needed his cooperation. The last thing she wanted to do was clean a damn refrigerator on top of everything else.

"Twenty."

"Boy, you must be on hard drugs. Where you think I get twenty dollars from?"

"I know you got money. You was with Larry and James last night, and I know at least one of them upped a few duckies." His smirk grew wider. He knew he had his sister in a bind. She'd give him the money because she could get more where that came from. "So, what's the deal?" he pressed.

"You need to get a job. I'm tired of being blackmailed by you."

"You giving me the money or what?" he asked.

"Ten dollars and not a cent more."

"Ten?" He contemplated it. "Do I get to hold the CDs?"

"Yeah. You make me sick with ya lazy ass."

"You still love me, though." He began dancing around the room to the rap song that blasted from his stereo.

"Do the cupid shuffle," he chanted. "To the left, to the left..."

"Toby, stop clowning."

"To the right to the right..."

"Toby, I'm trying to talk to you."

"What girl?" he asked. "You messing up my flow." He stopped dancing.

"You know you really ought to be in school," she said.

"Why? You don't go," he said. A defiant glint seeped into his eyes.

"I'm eighteen-years-old. You are only fourteen."

"So what? I hate school," he spat.

19

PROJECT QUEEN

"You didn't used to hate it. You were popular in middle school and then you get to high school, and you hate it? What happened?"

He shrugged. "I was the shit in middle school, but things were different in the ninth grade. The older kids picked on us all the time. I felt like punching niggas out."

"They do that to all the underclassmen. You'll get your turn next year when you become a sophomore," she said.

"No, I won't because I ain't going back to that bitch," he snapped.

He would never tell her how the kids taunted him about his no-name shoes and bargain store clothing. He wouldn't dare step foot in that school again to deal with that because he knew he would go off on any and everybody there.

"Then what you gonna do with the rest of ya life, huh? If you don't get an education, how you figure you gonna get out the projects?"

"How you gonna get out?" He threw the question back at her. He wanted to end the conversation. Thinking about how the kids had picked on him touched on a soft spot. It irritated him because he thought he was over all that.

"I'm a woman. I have what men want and they're willing to pay for it. That's how I'm getting out," she stated.

Toby threw back his head and laughed. "In that case, you ain't going nowhere. You gonna be a project ho 'til you die."

"You don't what you talking about, dumb ass." His insulting words cut into her. "You'll see. And it might be sooner than you think." She flounced out of his room, slamming the door behind her.

"Don't be slamming my door," he yelled. "Heifer."

Shae went into her own room and locked the door. She pulled up the carpet in one corner, reached underneath the padding, and retrieved the stash of money. It made her tingle when she counted out the tens, twenties, and even a few fifties. She'd conned all of it out of lovesick, dumb ass men. When she finished counting, she had close to fifteen hundred dollars. That wasn't bad, for *somebody else's* money.

With a self-satisfied smirk, she added another fifty dollars to the pile. She'd easily gotten James Wallace to give her thirty bucks when she let him fondle her breasts. She'd even gone so far as to let him suck on the delicate nipples. When he tried to go further, she made an excuse about it being that time of the month. With a disgusted look on his face, he'd pushed her away.

She'd gotten the other twenty from Larry Walker to buy some chicken from Churches. He'd been so drunk, she doubted he remembered giving her the money. Larry never expected anything in return. He was always a respectful, gentleman.

Shae remembered how James played with her breasts and it caused a warm sensation between her legs. James was extremely handsome and sexy as hell. She knew he wanted to get with her, but she wasn't ready to give up her virginity, especially not to anyone from the projects. She considered herself much too good for any of the neighborhood thugs.

Besides, James was twenty, and he still lived with his mama. He'd gotten several girls pregnant and would shack up with one or the other until they kick him out. Then, he'd go right back to his mama's place. He had no motivation, no skills, and seemed happy to drift from one dead-end job to the next.

No, she wasn't about to give in to James. It didn't matter to her how good looking he was or how he made her feel. The urge to have a hard, stiff dick would pass. If it got too intense, she could always rely on the vibrator she kept on the top shelf in her closet. It was a slim vibrator that she used to stimulate her clit. She'd occasionally insert it inside slowly, but not far enough to rupture her hymen. She didn't want to lose her virginity that way, so she was careful.

She felt like taking it out at that moment, but knew there wasn't enough time to get any real pleasure. She had too much to do, thanks to her fat ass mama.

She sighed, put the money back into its secret place and walked over to her jewelry box. In the little drawer, she kept a few bucks. She grabbed a five dollar bill and five ones for Toby. She really didn't care about giving him the money because she could always get more. She ignored the twinge between her legs and left the room.

CHAPTER TWO

After Shae left his room, Toby locked his door to make sure no one else would enter unannounced, like his mama. He didn't need the ten dollars that he got from his sister. He had plenty of money.

He pulled a shoebox from under his bed and lifted the lid. Money spilled over the edges, and a gun lay on top of the pile of cash.

He didn't know how he'd gotten mixed up in the dope gang and talked into selling drugs, but somehow that's exactly what happened. Now, he had to sell or face some serious consequences.

He sat on the edge of the bed and let his head fall into his hands. How could he get out the game without dying? He didn't want to sell drugs anymore. It had been all glitz and glamour for a minute, but now it had lost its appeal. Even though he would never admit it to Shae, he wished he could just go back to school and lead a normal life.

Shae wouldn't understand if he told her. She'd try to talk him out of it, as if it was that easy. And his mother had never been the kind of mother that he could confide in. Besides, if and when she found out, he would probably get the hell kicked out of him. He was determined not to let that happened.

His home life had prompted him to get involved with drugs in the first place. He began hanging out with some boys he went to school with just to get away from his mama. He'd been introduced to all kinds of drugs at a young age.

Before he could let common sense stop him, Toby began smoking marijuana and associating with drug dealers. He became the look out, alerting crack and weed dealers of anyone suspicious in the area.

23

PROJECT QUEEN

He figured selling drugs wasn't all that hard to do and the money was practically instant, so he dropped out of school to become a full time dealer. He wasn't worried about getting caught. Everybody he knew sold drugs and they never got caught. Even if he did get arrested, he'd receive a slap on the wrist. He could handle it.

He was rolling in the Benjamins, but he couldn't spend it freely or his mama would find out. And he'd be damned if he'd give it away. He spent a little here and there on girls, but knew all about gold digging tricks. They had their palms out so often they resembled collection plates. They desired fancy hairdos, expensive jewelry, and new clothes. They wanted some dumb ass busta who would pay their light bill or go half on the rent. A trick would settle for whatever she could get, but he wasn't a paymaster.

He'd never fall for their lame lines even though they threw themselves at him constantly. They shook their tits and jiggled their ass, encouraging him to touch them. Some had even gone so far as to show him their nookie – twerking it all up in his face, like that was going to change his mind. But, he wasn't ready for sex. He knew that he was handsome and had a nice physique at fourteen. Some grown women even lusted after him. He just wasn't ready to go that route. He felt that sex was overrated anyway, and he could wait.

Toby smiled wickedly as he thought about the women who'd tried to seduce him. He wouldn't go all the way, but he would let them give him a little slow smoking head, though. Even then, he made sure to use a condom. He wasn't about to catch anything from some nasty skank. Besides, he heard about how some women would suck a nigga dry but not swallow the semen. They'd go into the bathroom and use a turkey baster to insert the sperm into them in an effort to trap a nigga. He'd be damned if anyone would be able to walk around saying he was their baby's daddy. Being a teenaged father was the last thing he needed or wanted. When the time came, he knew how to protect himself. He had a top dresser drawer filled with Trojan condoms, just in case.

When Mrs. Byrts returned, Shae had taken the last basket of clothes out of the dryer. She'd cleaned the twins' room and remade the beds with fresh sheets and pillowcases. She'd vacuumed all the rooms and the hallway upstairs and had mopped the kitchen floor. The two bathrooms had been scrubbed clean: no ring around the tub, toothpaste or hair in the sink, and no smudges on the mirror. Shae made sure not to leave even a streak on the shower door. Something like that would cause Mrs. Byrts to flip out and have her redo everything.

Shae remembered one time when Toby didn't take out the garbage after he'd been told. Mrs. Byrts came home, saw the overflowing garbage can and became enraged. She picked up the garbage pail and dumped its contents on a sleeping Toby. After a few times of being awakened to the smell of funk, Toby learned to take the garbage out without being told.

Toby cleaned out the refrigerator because he knew how their mama could get. He felt kind of bad for his sister because she had to work like a slave. Cleaning the refrigerator was the least he could do.

Ma Violet washed, dried, and put the dishes away. The entire apartment was in order, but Mrs.

Byrts still frowned after gazing around. You would think she'd be happy, but she wasn't. Nothing ever seemed to please the woman. She complained about the living room not being vacuumed. Shae just rolled her eyes. What was wrong with her arms? As big as she was, she could easily pull a vacuum cleaner across the floor faster than Shae could do it.

"Toby, carry them groceries inside," she ordered. Toby, not up for a confrontation, complied. When he placed the last bag on the table, he turned toward his mama. He could tell she wasn't in a good mood, which was nothing new. She was ticking like a time bomb, and he wouldn't wait around for the explosion. Besides, he had things to do. He wasn't about to sit in the house like a prisoner of war and listen to his bitter mama's complaints. That was out. He didn't understand how his sister put up with it. In a few minutes, he would be missing in action, in places that even his mama wouldn't go.

Mrs. Byrts entered the kitchen as he flew by her in a flash and said, "Mama, I'm going to Doug's house." The front door closed behind him before she could respond.

"He must have a girlfriend he tryin' to get to, high tailin' it outta here like that," Ma Violet mused, chuckling.

"As long as he don't make no babies, he can have all the girlfriends he want," Mrs. Byrts said. "Shae put these groceries away. My back is hurting."

Shae frowned. Toby always did whatever he wanted and she got stuck with all the work. Pretty soon the twins would be home from school. She'd have to help them with their homework then cook dinner because her mother refused to cook for "*overgrown ass children*." That meant she'd have more

26

dishes to wash. Plus, she'd have to bathe her younger siblings and get them ready for bed.

Shae felt the anger building inside her, but choked it down. It wasn't the twins' fault that they had a fat, lazy ass mama. Maybe if Mrs. Byrts would get off the couch and do something...

After putting away the groceries, Shae went to her room. She couldn't stand it when her mama was home. She hogged the television in the living room, watching talk shows and *The Young & the Restless*. Shae hated soap operas and liked to watch B.E.T. all day. If she did happen to watch anything else, it had to be interesting. Most TV shows bored the hell out of her. In her opinion, none of them bordered on reality not even the reality television shows like *The Real World*. The projects, now that was *real*.

Shae wanted to go to her cousin's house, but knew that was out of the question. If her mama was home, she couldn't go anywhere. Even though she was eighteen, her mama treated her like a baby. The only times she got to go anywhere was when her mama went to work or out drinking. She kept wishing Mrs. Byrts would leave, but every time she went downstairs to check, she found her mama still parked on the couch.

She didn't dare ask permission to go over to Tashae's. If she did, then her mama would start ranting and raving, calling her all types of names like tramp, streetwalker, or ho. Mrs. Byrts constantly accused Shae of being a slut and compared her to Vivian. Vivian had gotten pregnant at age fifteen. Shae hadn't even had sex yet. But to let her mama tell it, she was the biggest ho in Jordan Park, in all of St. Petersburg.

Bored with staring at four walls Shae went outside to sit on the front porch. She watched the older students walking from their bus stops. It made her think about high school and what she was missing out on. Had she not quit, she'd be a senior. She'd probably be excited, looking forward to Grad Night, the prom and graduation. But, she'd been robbed of those memories because she dropped out in the tenth grade.

Her mother didn't even care that she stopped going to school. Since Shae would be home all day, she'd been ordered to take care of the twins. She'd done that until they got old enough to attend pre-school.

Now, she stared at the teenagers with envy. They all looked so happy and carefree. Some of the girls stood in short skirts with their legs shiny from lotion, gazing at the boys who stood a few feet away. The boys with zigzag braids or low cut fades talked animatedly about their latest CDs or video games. A few lagged behind, smoking. She wondered if any of them had to take care of their younger siblings every day. Did their mamas get drunk, cuss them out and beat them all the time?

Another large, yellow bus pulled to a noisy stop and more students shuffled off. Shae saw curious faces pressed up against the windows gazing at her. When the bus drove off, she felt a deep sadness and sighed. Maybe one day she'd be able to go back to school or get a GED. She knew she had to do something.

"Shae," her mama called through the screen door.

"Ma'am?"

"Bring ya ass in here and help ya grandma to the bathroom."

Shae gritted her teeth. Why did she have to help? She didn't understand why Mrs. Byrts couldn't do it herself. Her mother was the certified nursing assistant and worked as a home health aide. She just shook her head, got up and went inside to do her mother's bidding.

At a quarter after three the door burst open and in ran the twins. They immediately began to demand things until Shae stopped them with a glare.

"Charles and Chris, go upstairs, get out of ya school clothes, then come on back down and watch cartoons until I get dinner ready," she instructed. They knew better than to disobey her because she would grab a belt and wear their behinds out. They could sense her anger and thought they caused it because of the soiled sheets. They went up the stairs quietly. Five minutes later, they trudged back down with freshly scrubbed hands and faces. She hadn't had to tell them to do it.

They didn't dare argue over which cartoons to watch as they usually did. The boys knew from experience that the slightest thing could set their sister's temper off. Neither of them wanted to feel the sting of the belt. But, they'd rather get a spanking from Shae than from their mother on any given day.

Shae noticed Charles take a sideways glance at their mother who sat on the couch. He didn't want to chance making her angry. Most of the time, she just ignored them unless they did something she felt warranted a beating. Then, she'd attack them viciously with whatever she could lay her hands on.

At times like that, Shae would intervene and usually ended up taking the brunt of the beating. She couldn't stand to watch her mother punish the twins because the woman had no mercy.

Thankfully, nothing happened to unleash her fury. That day, she seemed almost happy. She'd even bought some powdered donuts that she gave to Ma Violet and the twins. From the kitchen, Shae glared at her in resentment. She really couldn't stand the woman.

Once she'd prepared dinner, Shae called the twins to the table. They sat down, said Grace, and began to eat. She had fried some chicken wings, cooked rice and heated up some canned corn. Charles and Chris loved chicken, so they didn't complain. Truthfully, they were good boys and rarely complained about anything. Shae didn't understand why their mother treated them like redheaded stepchildren.

"Mama, can I go to the store?" she finally asked, needing to get out and stretch her legs.

"Go 'head," Mrs. Byrts grunted.

"Don't let them brats go in my room," she said.

"If they go in there, that's they damn business," she replied. "Should lock ya do'" Mrs. Byrts replied.

"What I gotta lock it for? They should just stay out. It won't stay locked anyway. All they have to do is shake on it and it'll pop open."

"What you got in there that's so important?" Ma Violet tooted. Shae didn't bother to answer her.

"Jus' go to the store and stop nagging," Mrs. Byrts snapped. "If they go in ya room, beat they asses. Shit. Just leave me the fuck alone about it. Ok?"

Shae sighed. She'd grown tired of being the one to discipline the twins. They weren't *her* children. It seemed like her mother had forgotten that fact. She loved her brothers and didn't want to hurt one of them. It could happen. Each day it got harder to cope with all of the pressure, not to mention her mother's attitude. She got yelled at and cursed out constantly as well as belittled on a daily basis.

Shae could understand why Vivian left when she turned sixteen. She wondered where Vivian had gone and felt a sudden sadness. Vivian had run off and freed herself, and she was still left behind in hell.

"Thought you said you was going to the store?" Her mom's voice cut into her thoughts.

"I am," she snapped. *Vivian is lucky she got away* she thought as she squinted at her mother, feeling something close to hatred burn in her chest.

"Bring me back one of them pickled, pig feet and a two liter bottle of Pepsi. Get some instant oatmeal for ya grandma's breakfast," the woman demanded. "And get another box of powdered donuts, too. This one 'bout empty."

"Didn't you just go grocery shopping?"

"And?"

"Don't seem like it," she said. Shae sucked air between her teeth.

"You must not want to leave this house," Mrs. Byrts threatened, eyes narrowing. "Get what I told you to get."

"Okay." Shae hurried out the door, grumbling under her breath. She couldn't wait to get out of there so she could breathe.

Once outside, she could immediately feel the men's eyes bore into her and it boosted her ego. She might be nothing in her mother's eyes, but out in the

31

streets, she could be anyone she wanted. She felt beautiful and desirable. She felt like a queen.

"Hey, Shae, wait up." She turned when someone called her and saw Larry Walker. Shae felt apprehensive, but Larry just smiled when he approached her. She knew that if he was upset about her taking his money last night, he wouldn't be cheesing in her face now.

"What's up?" he greeted. "Girl, you sure look good. Good enough to eat." He laughed. Larry had a medium complexion. He was well built for a guy of eighteen. He fell in-between cute and handsome because of a birthmark that covered a great portion of the left side of his face. It was much lighter than the rest of his skin and it stood out. He had beautiful, soul-searching brown eyes.

"What's up Larry?" she asked. For some reason, she always felt happy when she saw him. She couldn't remember a day since she'd met him in the second grade that he hadn't been around.

"Not much. I was heading to the store. Seem like you headed in the same direction. Mind if a nigga like me tag along?"

"Larry, you know I don't mind."

"Just making sure. I mean, you all beautiful and shit. I don't want none of this ugliness to rub off on ya."

"Larry, you know I don't like hearing you talk like that. Stop putting yourself down."

Larry threw her a surprised look. He'd never heard her speak like that before. In the past when he made negative comments about his looks, she'd add to it. He'd expected her to say something like, "You ain't ugly, but that spot covering half ya face is." Momentarily speechless, he just looked at Shae.

"You ok?" he asked, finally finding his voice.

"Yeah. Why?"

"I don't know. You just seem different or something."

"Nah. I'm ok," she assured. "I just had an argument with my mama again. She gets on my fucking nerves."

"Oh?" Larry fell silent. Once again, Shae had shocked him. He'd never heard her talk negatively about her family. Until that moment, he'd thought everything was perfect.

"I can't wait to get out of here," she went on. "These damn projects make my ass itch."

"I know what you mean. I have an opportunity to break free and I'm gonna take it."

"You don't live *in* the projects," she reminded.

"I might as well," he said bitterly. He lived directly across the street from them. He associated with project folk most of his life. All of his friends lived there. He considered himself just as hood and ghetto as the next nigga from the projects.

"What you gonna do, start selling drugs?" The question came out like an accusation. She stopped walking and glared at him, waiting for his response.

"Hell no, girl. I ain't with that shit. That'll fuck a nigga's life up. Besides, after what happened to my mama–" His voice trailed off and he looked angrier than she'd ever seen him. "Hell no," he repeated, shaking his head. "I'm getting out the clean way. I'm going to college, to the Art Institute of Fort Lauderdale. I just found out today that I got a full art scholarship." He looked down at his feet as if embarrassed to share the information.

"That shit is tight, Larry," she congratulated. "I'm happy for you." They continued to walk.

33

"Thanks," he mumbled graciously. He hadn't told anyone else. He'd wanted to share the news with Shae first. That's why he'd been heading to her place when he ran into her.

"At least you ain't wasting ya talents. I wish I was smart like you or could draw or something," she said.

"You got a talent, Shae. You just don't know what it is yet- and it ain't sex," he said.

"I know that. I just can't do anything. School bored the hell out of me. That's why I quit." Larry didn't bother asking her to elaborate. They had walked to the bus stop together every morning since second grade. During their tenth grade year, she'd started acting different, missing days, looking tired, dragging. Suddenly, one day, Shae stopped coming altogether. After about a week, he stopped by her place to find out if something had happened to her. She informed him that she wasn't going back to school. When he questioned her at the time, she damn near cursed him out. He left it alone then, just as he was going to do now.

"What do you like doing?" he asked, instead.

She sighed in frustration. "I don't know. For some reason, I just like counting money. I know it sounds silly, but I picture myself working at a bank and counting money. It's stupid. I don't even have a high school diploma. I ain't gonna be working at nobody's bank anytime soon," she said.

"No, it's not stupid," he told her. "It's a vision and visions ain't stupid. My aunt says that we should write down our visions and they'll come into being," he told her. "Whatever you set ya mind to, you can do it. You are too damn pretty and smart to just waste away in a place like the projects."

They reached the store, which had been converted from an old gas station. Men sat around a rickety card table playing Spades, smoking cigars, drinking Colt 45 and Budweiser. Others stood around watching the game. They all stopped momentarily to stare lustfully at Shae when she approached.

"Hot damn. Tenderoni," one man yelled. "Will you be my wife?" Everybody laughed and hooted. Larry didn't find it amusing at all. He ushered Shae into the store.

"Man, is that you?" a teenager heading out asked him as he surveyed Shae with appreciation. "Girl, is ya husband married?" he whispered to Shae.

"Man, what the fuck you looking at?" Larry challenged. "Yeah, she my lady."

The guy threw up his hands. "Calm down, man. I was just asking." He jumped on his bicycle, pedaling off.

"That nigga on a bike and trying to holla. Why would you want a broke pimp?"

Shae laughed. "Why did you lie to that boy?"

"Just made myself feel good. I wish I could have a lovely girl like you. That's an impossible dream." Shae just smiled and walked ahead of him. She cared about Larry more than he knew. But, some things were better left unsaid.

Shae's ass immediately enraptured the old man behind the counter. He failed to notice three kids stuffing candy bars under their shirts. Larry caught wind of it though and chuckled.

"Yo Pops, EBP?" Larry asked when the man continued to eye Shae up and down. He was smacking his lips like he was getting ready for a tasty treat.

35

"W-what was that, boy?" The man stopped staring at Shae and turned his attention to Larry.

"I said, EBP?" Larry repeated.

"What's that, some new kinda drug?" he asked in a suspicious tone. "Ain't gonna be none of that up in here, son."

"No, it means, do you have an *eye ball problem*? I see you sweating my lady. What's up?" He held up his hands in a questioning gesture.

"Aw boy, all I can do is look." He waved Larry off good-naturedly. "I'm too damn old to do anythin' else. No harm intended. You got ya self one fine young lady." He leaned closer to Larry and lowered his voice. "You got that yet?" he whispered.

"Got what yet?"

"You know what I'm talkin' 'bout boy. You ain't dumb, is ya?"

"Old man, you a border line perv. Do you order women's panties on-line?" He saw Shae walking toward the front of the store. "Hey Shae, guess what this man just asked me?"

"What?" Shae placed the items she'd gotten on the counter top.

"You don't even wanna know." Larry laughed. "He asked me if I got me some yet?"

"That ain't his fucking business," Shae said. The kids that had been stealing stood at the front of the store edging toward the door. They giggled loudly. The man paused from ringing up Shae's items and pointed at them.

"Y'all sticky fingered lil bastards, get on outta my store," he yelled. They gave him the finger and ran out. He leaned over the counter, craning his neck to yell behind them. "I knows all ya folks. Don't get it twisted." He turned back to Shae as if he hadn't

36

stopped talking to her at all. "I know it ain't my business, but you sho look mighty fine. Mighty fine."

"Stop foaming at the mouth and finish ringing her up," Larry snapped. He didn't care if the man had one foot in the grave; he was flirting with *his* woman.

"Alright. Alright. You ain't gotta yell. Shit. Fucking young ass fuckerss these days ain't got no damn respect," he mumbled as he threw the stuff into a brown paper bag.

"What's up, old man? You want me to come cross this damn counter?" Larry challenged. Shae knew that he was joking, but she wasn't sure if the old man knew.

"Larry, come on and stop messing with that man. He might have a heart attack," she said.

"Only thing gone make me have a heart attack is you, Sugar," the man responded, winking at Shae. "I'll try that Viagra drug for you. You one fine, sweet young thing. Make a man like me wish he was fifty years younger."

"Please. If you was fifty years younger, you'd still be about sixty," she said. She grabbed her purchases and sashayed away.

"Grandpa got a lot of nerves, trying to hit on me. He'd probably give me worms," she said. Larry laughed.

"Besides, you're not in the market for a sugar *grand*daddy." He shook his head. "Girl, if you belonged to me, I'd have to lock you up. You get too much attention. I'd be *too* jealous."

They watched as a white Chevy Caprice pulled up in front of the store. It was eye-catching, with spinning rims and loud music blasting from the amps in the trunk.

37

"Damn Red." The guy on the passenger's side leaned out the window. He had big teeth and resembled the actor that played JJ on *Good Times.* "What's yo name?" He ignored Larry who scowled at him.

"Come on, Shae. You don't need to mix with them kind of people," Larry said lowly.

"Go on Larry. I'll catch up with you. I won't be but a few minutes." Larry stood there with a defiant look on his face. "Go on, shit. I ain't no damn baby needing to be watched," she snapped.

With reluctance, Larry headed off. He moved slowly and looked back several times. Finally, he just threw up his hands and walked at a normal pace. He turned the corner and was out of sight.

"What's up, Red? What's yo name?" the guy asked again.

"I'm Shae. Who wants to know?" she answered.

"What you 'bout Red? Like having a good time?"

"That depends on what kind of a good time you talking 'bout."

"You know, sniffing a lil powder, getting high?" the guy said.

"No. I ain't with it." She walked off.

"Hey wait." She heard a different voice and turned around. The driver had been hidden behind his partner, blocked from her view. "Can you step 'round here to my side for a minute?" he asked.

"Hell nah."

"Girl, stop trippin'. My dawg said step to him."

"So? He ain't God. He wanna say something to me, he can get out the car."

"Obviously, you don't know who I am," the driver spoke again. He nudged his friend aside and she got a clear look at him.

"No. Is that supposed to scare me?" she asked, glaring at him. He held her gaze. She had to admit he was one of the most handsome men she'd ever laid eyes on. Her heart pounded crazily in her chest.

"Get in the car." His eyes seemed to hypnotize her. Against her will, she moved toward the Chevy.

"Wait a minute. I don't even know you," she said, stepping back.

"You will." It sounded like a promise. Shae looked away and gained some control.

"I have to go. My mama's waiting on me to get back with this stuff." She indicated the bag she held.

"I'll take you home. Where you live?" She didn't answer right away. "Where was that?"

"The projects," she finally said.

"The projects," the other guy exclaimed. "As fine as you is? Damn."

"Yeah. What of it? Y'all got something against the projects?" she asked.

"No. I don't," the driver answered. "I go there to conduct business all the time. By the way, my name is Dana. Dana Russell."

"Better known as D.D.D.," Mouth said.

"What?"

"Diamond Dog Dana." If the car hadn't convinced her of the danger, now the red flags went up. With a name like that, he *had* to be a drug dealer. Yeah, she just bet he *conducted business* in the projects. Shae couldn't be bothered with a low-down drug dealer. All of them were male-whores that slept with everything on the block, street, or corner. Chicken heads, dirty-foots, maggots, scallywags: a drug dealer didn't care who he let lick his balls. Her opinion of them was just as worse as her opinion of male strippers.

39

"Well, it was nice meeting you, Dana. I gotta go. See you around," she said.

"Wait. Can't I get a number?" Dana asked.

"No phone," she tossed over her shoulder.

"Can you give me an address? Somethin'?" he pleaded.

"Just come to Jordan Park and ask for Shae. You'll find me if you really want to," she said, hurrying off before the guy could stop her again.

Larry sat on the porch and waited for Shae to arrive. His fists clenched and unclenched. Why did she want to stay behind and converse with some no-account drug dealer? No good would come of that; he was sure of it.

When she got there, he scowled her way. "It took you long enough," he said.

"Since when did you become my daddy?" She placed her hands on her hips and glared at him.

"I'm just trying to watch ya back. Girl, that nigga is a notorious drug dealer. You have no idea how ruthless he can be," he said.

"I can take care of myself," she told him. "Besides, it ain't none of ya business." Larry's head dropped and his bottom lip jutted out causing her to feel a stab of regret. She knew that he was soft on her, and she didn't want to hurt him in any way. When she actually thought about it, he really was the only real friend she had. Oh, there was James. Unlike James, Larry never tried to get between her legs.

She shifted her weight from one foot to the other. Should she apologize? He was always so nice to her and she really appreciated his friendship. "Larry,

I'm—sorry," she said. "Give me a minute to take this stuff to my mama and I'll be right back."

He gave her a quick glance, nodded then looked away. Any moment that he got to spend with her was priceless. He didn't know if he could let her know that though.

When Shae went inside, her grandmother came out.

"Hello, young man," she said.

"Hey Ma Violet. How you doing this evening?" he asked.

"I can't complain. Blessed. Just wonderfully blessed," she said, sitting down in a chair near the door. "So, you determined to make Shae fall fer ya, ain't ya?" she asked.

Larry laughed, as his face flushed. He didn't know if he should answer her out-of-the-blue question. "I think that's impossible. She and I are just friends." He exhale and averted his eyes.

"I can tell you wish it was somethin' more. Hmff. If you didn't care 'bout that girl, you wouldn't keep comin' back for the abuse." She cackled like a hen and Larry shook his head. Ma Violet was so right in her assessment. No matter what Shae said or did, he always wanted to be around her.

When Shae returned, Larry could barely look at her. What if she figured out how he felt? Was he walking around wearing his heart on his sleeve? If Ma Violet could see it, maybe Shae could too.

He wondered if she knew from the first day back in elementary school. He met her in the second grade when he moved to St. Petersburg from Philadelphia. He fell in love at first sight. She'd looked so pretty with her long pigtails and fair-colored skin. She wore a blue, frilly dress with white bobby socks and shiny

41

black shoes. Looking at her had melted his heart. To him, she resembled a delicate, china doll. From day one, he wanted to protect her.

During recess on that first day of class, he found out that she wasn't delicate at all. And she definitely didn't need anyone to protect her. She'd proven that she was tough as nails when she whipped a boy named Billy's butt after he pushed her out of the swing.

Once the fight ended, she gazed down at her skinned knee. All the other kids gathered around Billy, taunting him. Larry didn't care about teasing some sissy who got beat up by a girl. It served him right.

Instead, he went over to where Shae sat on the ground and inspected her wound.

"Does it hurt?" he asked.

"Of course it hurts, stupid." Her eyelids blinked rapidly as she fought back tears.

"Well, I have a Band Aid. You want it?"

"Why you carry 'round Band Aids?"

"I don't," he said quickly. He didn't want her to think he was a weirdo. "I jus' happen to have one 'cause my finger got cut." He'd held up a wrapped index finger and wiggled it.

"Okay. Give it to me. And hurry up."

"You sure are bossy. But, I like you." She gazed at him quizzically then her mouth turned upwards. He retrieved the Band Aid from his pocket, opened it, and gingerly placed it on her sore knee. He helped her up, and they'd walked into the building together.

Back in the classroom, the kids teased them and sang: "Shae and Larry, sitting in a tree K- I- S- S- I- N G..." Shae blushed down to her roots and Larry felt a warm sensation wash over him. Neither of them demanded that their classmates stop chanting the song. They just stared at each other with silly grins on their faces.

Yes, Larry thought as he reminisced. He looked over at Shae who sat next to her grandmother. His eyes softened. *I've loved Shae for as long as I can remember.* He never got up the nerve to tell her, though. He figured if he hung around her long enough she'd get the message. Ten years later, she still seemed to have no clue. Since he'd be leaving soon, he felt he should reveal his true feelings.

CHAPTER THREE

To the windows! To the walls! 'Til the sweat drop down my..."
The thin walls of the apartment vibrated.
"God, Toby. Turn that music down. People can't even sleep." Shae groaned and rolled over. The alarm clock on the nightstand read 5:14 AM. *What the hell he doing up this damn early?*" she mumbled and reluctantly got out of bed. She found the robe she'd flung on a chair earlier and slipped it on.

"Get low! Get low! Get low!" The song continued to pound into her head. Her face tightened as she stumbled toward Toby's room.

She charged in without knocking. "Toby, what's yo problem, boy? You know people trying to sleep this time-" Her hand flew up to her mouth and her eyes widened. Marijuana and cocaine covered the bed spread.

Toby jumped, causing some drug paraphernalia to fall off the bed. "Man, you forgot how to knock?" he yelled. He didn't bother covering up the drugs.

"What you doing with this shit? So, you gonna start selling drugs like the next common thug, right?"

"I ain't just started- I *been* doing this So what? Just mind ya own business," he told her. "Touch ya nose." Now Shae understood why Toby could afford the latest urban wear and the newest, most expensive shoes.

"What the fuck wrong with you and this noise early this morning?" Mrs. Byrts' voice boomed louder than the music. She parked herself in the doorway, leaning against the doorjamb. She held a glass filled with brown liquor and ice.

44

Toby's mouth opened, forming a circle. He unsuccessfully tried to pull the comforter over the drugs before she saw them.

"Toby, what is that?" she asked. Her eyes swept the floor where the small plastic baggies littering it. "And what's under that bedspread, boy?"

"I, uh, I c-can explain," he stammered.

"Just shut ya damn mouth. You must think I'm a fool or something. I can see what's going on. I ain't blind." Her eyes were cold and hard. "You know damn well I don't play this shit. You must have lost what lil fucking brains God gave you." She entered the room, threw back the cover, and picked up some of the crack. "Look at this shit." Before Toby could blink, she caught him upside the head with an open hand slap. "No, you didn't start this. You taking ya ass back to school. That's what you gone do and I mean that. Now get this shit out of my house."

Toby kicked the edge of the bed. He gathered up the drugs and paraphernalia from the floor.

"Big ass bitch," he mumbled, low enough for only Shae to hear.

"What the fuck did you say?" Mrs. Byrts screeched. Her eyes turned red. "It ain't gonna take too much mo' for me to get on ya ass. So, ya best bet is to shut ya fucking mouth. I will rearrange this room up with ya sorry ass." Shae felt the fear that always came when their mother went on one of her rampages. In the end, someone always ended up hurt. She prayed that Toby would just be quiet before he ended up getting tossed to the floor and kicked unmercifully.

"Mama, I'm tired of you yelling and cussing at me all the time," Toby yelled. "You always telling me what the hell I can and can't do, and I'm sick of it."

"Toby, what's wrong with you?" Shae asked. Her eyes darted from Toby to Mrs. Byrts. Mrs. Byrts face tightened, turned a few shades darker, and the hand not holding the glass clenched into a fist. A large jugular vein throbbed.

"Ain't nothing wrong with me. I'm just sick of this shit. I'm tired of living in these sorry ass, roach infested projects. I'm tired of being poor." His eyes narrowed before he continued. "Mama, something's wrong with you. You ain't like nobody else's mama I know. It's one thing for kids to get beatings, but hell, we get *beat downs*. That's messed up. It ain't supposed to happen."

Shae inhaled, anticipating their mother's wrath. Mrs. Byrts just shook her head. "Look, you can stand here and run ya mouth all you want," she said, "but you getting out of here with that mess. I'm not going to jail behind ya sorry ass. And if you get me kicked off of Section 8 because of this, I will tear up the sidewalk with ya ass."

Shae's brow lifted. Was that it? All she was going to do was give Toby a slap on the wrist? But, he was selling drugs. "Mama, tell him not to sell drugs," Shae pleaded.

Mrs. Byrts had already turned back to nursing her drink. Ice clinked against the empty glass. "I can't make that hardheaded boy listen. He just like Vivian." With that, she turned and left the room. The slam of the door reverberated in their ears.

Shae stood, mouth wide opened. She still couldn't believe Toby had escaped their mother's fury. Not only had he brought drugs into the house, he'd been totally disrespectful to her.

"You got off lucky," she said. "Mama must be too tired or hung-over from hanging out last night and drinking."

"So what? I ain't scared of her." Yet, his voice cracked and he visible trembled.

Shae felt that Toby couldn't possibly understand the danger of what he was doing. Selling drugs could not become a career choice for him.

"Toby, don't throw your life away," she said. "You are too smart for that. Go back to school. Finish your education. Be somebody."

"I *am* somebody right now," he said. "Shae, I know what I'm doing. Just stop nagging me, will you? I can handle this." He broadened his shoulder and stuck out his chest. But, she still saw a lost little boy standing before her.

"It's your life." Toby put the cocaine and marijuana into a large, zip lock bag. A knot formed in her chest as he walked past and down the stairs.

Shae tried to go back to sleep but couldn't. After tossing and turning for the next hour, she groaned and sat up. Thirty minutes later, there were grits, eggs, sausage, hash browns, and pancakes on the table for Ma Violet and the twins. Shae tried to swallow down scrambled eggs, but they only got lodged in her throat. She couldn't shake the enormous sense of dread she felt.

Larry joined Shae on her front porch. He lowered his voice. "So, ya brother is in the gang, I heard?" Shae remained silent. "Booney and them was talking about it the other day. I can't believe

Toby would get mixed up in something like that." He shook his head.

"Yeah," she mumbled. "Me neither." She fidgeted in her seat. "I don't really want to talk about it."

Larry attempted light-heartedness. "Well, it's better for him to be selling drugs instead of using."

"That's not funny. Just shut up. I said I didn't want to talk about it."

"Hey, sor—ry."

They both grew silent and watched some people across from them try to start a fire on a charcoal grill. At first, it didn't catch, but one man kept squeezing lighter fluid on the coals. When it finally caught, a big "whoosh" had everyone backing off in a hurry.

"Now, that's a fire!" someone yelled, and they all cracked up.

James Wallace ambled up the sidewalk. He paused to watch the men messing with the grill. He shook his head, laughing. When he saw Shae and Larry, he went over.

"What's up?" he greeted.

"Ain't nothing much," Larry replied as they slapped hands. Shae chose to ignore him. He gave her a puzzled look, shook his head, and sat down. He just couldn't figure her out. One day, she was letting him suck on her tits, the next she was giving him attitude. Women. He loved them madly, but could do without the PMS.

"Y'all heard about ya boy, Chancey?" he asked.

"Nah, what happened?" Larry asked.

"Somebody capped that nigga last night. They found him in an alley with a bullet in his head. His car was all shot up, too. You know he used to sell crack, then he started using. He always ended up

48

smoking more than he sold. Somebody said he fucked up and smoked the wrong nigga's shit. When he couldn't come up with the cash, he got offed. "

"Damn. That's fucked you. But, I guess that's how it is in the world of drugs," Larry said.

"I know what you mean." James got quiet, his forehead creased in thought.

"What's wrong, man?" Larry asked. "You're concentrating mighty hard. It must hurt."

"Nothing. Well—I'm leaving here next week," he said.

"What?" Both Larry and Shae asked.

"I'm heading out," he told them. "I joined the Army." They stared at him, speechless. James took it to mean that they didn't believe him. "I'm serious. I'll be leaving next Tuesday. Ain't nothing here for me in these projects. This ain't no kinda life." He shook his head, looking at the men cooking on the grill. He wanted so much more for himself than to end up like those losers. All they did was sit around gambling, smoking, and drinking. Occasionally they'd argue and fight. When things were going well, they had cookouts. There had to be more to life than that. A grown ass man should have his own and not live in the projects with his mama.

He knew he'd been half-stepping. Since he'd graduated from high school, he hopped from one meaningless job to the next. He also went from one woman to the next. Now, he'd fathered more children than he cared to admit.

"I know what you mean," Larry agreed. "Soon as school is out, I'll be heading to Ohio myself."

"I been thinking 'bout it for a long time," James continued, ignoring Larry's news. It hadn't slipped past Shae, though. Her heart seemed to skip a beat and suddenly it grew difficult for her to breathe. She found it hard to continue listening to the conversation.

"I have three, possibly four kids, and I'm not even twenty-one. I want to be able to take care of mine. I don't want them living like I have." He'd watched his mama struggle since before he could remember. She had little education and worked many dead-end jobs just to take care of him and his three sisters. All her money went toward keeping the bills paid. She never had anything left over to do much with. She was in her late forties and didn't have anything that she could call her own. It seemed to him that all her hard work over the years had been for nothing. When she died, she wouldn't have anything she could leave to her kids, except unpaid debts.

He didn't want to end up like that. He wanted to have something he could pass on to his children. He needed a legacy. The Army would enable him to have that.

"I know what you mean," Larry repeated, still slightly shocked. They all fell silent, each thinking their own thoughts.

"So, Shae?" James broke the silence. "Can a brother finally get some before he leaves?" he asked.

"Go to hell." She got up and went inside, letting the screen door slam behind her.

"What's up with her?" James asked. "I was just joking."

"She's upset about Toby selling drugs. Don't try her like that, man." Larry suddenly felt protective of Shae. James was always taking things too far.

"Since when did you become her watch dog?"

Irritation crept into his voice. "Me and Shae go way back. You know that," he answered.

"What's up, nigga? Are you getting soft on Shae or something?" He laughed when Larry didn't answer. "Aw, man you got it bad."

"Whatever."

James wouldn't drop the subject. Instead, he began to sing:

"I've been there, done it, humped around
After all that - this is what I found
Nobody wants to be alone
If you're touched by the words in this song
Then maybe...
U got, u got it bad"

"Man, fuck you." Larry got up and followed Shae inside. As usual, Ma Violet sat in her rocker by the window. "Hello Ma Violet."

She nodded. "Hey, baby. How you doing?"

James entered. "Hi Ma Violet," he said. Ma Violet snorted and turned up her nose. The wooden chair squeaked as she rocked, watched, and listened. She'd heard what he asked her granddaughter and didn't appreciate it one bit.

Mannish lil demon, she thought.

"Man, why don't she like me?" James whispered to Shae, sitting on the couch next to her.

"I don't know," she answered. The truth was, she really didn't care. At that moment, she couldn't stand him too much herself. It dawned on her that James had always been annoying. The only reason she put up with him was because he was a paymaster. Now, she hated the fact that she'd ever let him touch her. There wasn't enough money in the world that could convince her to sleep with his trifling behind.

51

"You know ya arms too short to box with grandma," Larry joked. The two of them doubled over. Shae's scowl cut their laughter short.

James frowned. "Shae, ya sour mood is getting on my nerves. The last time I ran into you at the store, you had an attitude. Hell, I'm not the one responsible for you problems, so why are taking it out on me? You been walking 'round with ya ass on ya shoulder all week. Damn," he complained.

"It's my ass," she told him.

"What's bugging you? You PMSing or something?"

"None of ya damn business. If you don't like the way I'm acting, then step."

"Shit, I will. I don't have to take this." He was through tiptoeing around her. She acted like she was the only female that had a vagina. Well, it wasn't like she was giving any to him. She was a big tease. He was still pissed off about her giving him blue balls the other night. "I get aggravated enough from other nappy headed hoes." He stood.

Shea jumped up, too. "You calling me a nappy headed ho?"

"Come on, Shae. Chill out," Larry intervened. "James, you too, man." They both ignored him.

"If you a ho, you a ho. Simple as that. Don't matter if you nappy headed or not," James snarled.

"Keep talking shit and I'll show you what a ho can do."

"Bitch, you don't scare me." James pointed in her face.

"Wait a minute! Chill out!" Larry got up and stood between the two. "James, there you go taking things too far again, man. You don't have to be disrespectful."

James' lips twisted. "Fuck you, nigga. She got you whipped and you ain't never getting in the panties."

Larry's face darkened. "James, don't try me." He'd let too much slide and now his anger was evident.

James knew he'd instigated the situation, but pride wouldn't let him back down. "What's up? You wanna do something? Bring it on then, nigga."

"Look, James, I don't want to fight you. This is stupid. Why you tripping and shit, man? We dawgs. I thought we was down?" Larry tried to appeal to the years of friendship between them. It must have worked because James threw up his hands and backed off.

"Fuck it. I'm out. I'm going where I can get with a real female, not some stuck-up, tight ho like that. Both of y'all can kiss my black ass." He left in a huff, letting the door slam.

"Nasty mouth buzzard," Ma Violet said. "Should of got rid of him a long time ago. He ain't no darn good. I hope the Army teach him some respect."

Shae and Larry looked at each other and exploded with laughter.

"Ma Violet a trip," Larry said. Shae shook her head in agreement. The things that James said had gotten under her skin, and she wanted to forget them.

"She's only speaking the truth, though."

"Ma Violet don't sugarcoat nothing. She tells it like it is." Larry shook his head. "I hope the Army molds that nigga into a man. He'll get his ass kicked trying me."

"Whatever Larry. You're a lover, not a fighter." Shae laughed.

"Yeah, you're right about that." He wanted to say, "I'll fight for you." Instead he changed the subject. "You got anything cold to drink?"

"What do you want?"

"I want some good old red Kool-Aid."

"You know I don't drink that shit." Shae said, heading for the kitchen. "How about a soda?"

"That'll work."

She handed him a Pepsi and sat down next to him on the couch. They watched television for a while. Ma Violet had long since nodded off in her rocking chair.

"Hey, ya grams fell asleep. Can you change off *the Golden Girls*?" Larry asked.

"I don't feel like watching TV anymore. You want to go up to my room and listen to some CDs?"

"Yeah, okay. That's cool."

"I got that new Lil Wayne."

"Do you have 50 Cent's new one, too?"

"Yeah, I think so. You know how I am with music. I buy everything," she said. "Come on."

Larry followed her up the stairs. As she walked, he checked her out. He couldn't help himself. She wore a South Pole jeans jumpsuit and she looked sexy as hell in it.

"What's that smell?" he exclaimed when they reached the top of the stairway.

"It's pee. The twins wet their beds again." Shae turned up her nose. "I let the windows up to air it out but I guess it didn't work."

"Smell like a damn possum got loose and got carried away. Better Febreze that mug."

Shae couldn't hold back her laughter. Larry always cracked her up. He was a comedian in his

54

own right and could probably run a ring around Chris Tucker.

She opened the door to her room. As they entered, Larry gazed around. He'd only been in Shae's room once, so he marveled at the changes. "What them niggas doing hanging on ya wall?" He referred to various posters of Shemar Moore and Dwayne "The Rock" Johnson. "I should be hanging right on the ceiling." He gazed up and caught his reflection in the tiny mirrors. "I *am* on the ceiling. That's tight." He sat down on the bed before Shae had the opportunity to remove a stack of clean underwear she'd folded earlier. When he noticed her gaze and apparent embarrassment, he grabbed a pair of g-strings and held them up.

"Wow." He whistled. He felt his nature rise just thinking about Shae wearing the sexy under-garments. "I guess it ain't Victoria's secret no more." He wiggled the garment on the end of his index finger.

"Larry, stop." She snatched them away from him. She quickly grabbed the rest and tucked them into a drawer. "What do you want to listen to first?" she asked.

"Don't matter," he stated. He picked up an *Essence* magazine and thumbed through it. Shae put a Toni Braxton CD in the stereo. "Why do you read this trash?" He tossed the magazine toward the garbage can. "Trash. That's what it is."

"Don't be throwing my stuff away," she chastised and retrieved the magazine. She placed it on top of others that rested on a nightstand.

"I see you got quite a music collection." He got up and went over to browse through her CDs. "Play this one," he said holding it up like an excited child.

"Which one?" she asked.

"Usher." James had been right, he *did* have it bad.

"Usher? I don't want to hear him right now. All he do is whine."

"Whine? Oh no. Keith Sweat whines, not Usher."

"Yes he does. Ever since Chili dumped his ass, he whines and cries on just about every song he got now."

"Aw man, that's cold. Chili didn't dump him. They mutually agreed to part ways."

"She gave that nigga the boot. I would have, too, if he'd gone behind my back and got another ho pregnant."

"Hey, that's just hearsay. Gossip. Regardless, I still want to hear him. Play the damn CD, woman."

"Nope," she refused.

"Come on, Shae. I'm your company. You're supposed to let company have their way. I'm a guest."

"Too bad." She playfully snatched the CD out of his hands.

"Give that back. I'm going to hear it, one way or another." He tried to take it back from her. They wrestled each other toward the bed. "Shae, give me the CD." They stumbled at the edge of the bed, falling onto it. Larry landed on top of Shae.

Suddenly, the CD seemed unimportant. Larry gazed into Shae's lovely face, completely mesmerized. She didn't try to push him off her, and he made no move to get up.

"Larry, st-" she began. The sentence got cut off when he leaned forward and their lips met. Shae's body responded instantly. She moaned as Larry's tongue slipped into her mouth. A delicious feeling of

56

warmth coursed through her entire body. She could feel Larry's passion throbbing against her thigh, and it excited her.

"I want you," Larry all but groaned and kissed her again. His hands found her breasts, but he couldn't feel them through the thick material. He impatiently unzipped the front of the jumper and eased it from her shoulders. He trailed kisses along her collarbone and neck, stopping long enough to gaze into her eyes.

Shae looked dazed as she stared back at Larry. Her long hair cascaded around her shoulders. Her breasts strained against the flimsy material of her bra. He reached around and unhooked it and they sprang forth. Her erect nipples jutted out at him and he couldn't resist taking one into his mouth. The moan came from the back of her throat. She didn't protest when he raised her up and slipped the jumpsuit from her body. She was clothed in only a pair of g-string underwear, which didn't cover much.

"You are too sexy," he complimented. His hands shook when he touched her. He covered the other nipple with his warm mouth and she gasped. Never had she felt so hot. The pressure between her legs got so intense that it felt like she'd explode.

Larry worked on both nipples, alternating from the left to the right. He twirled his tongue around the tips then pulled them into his wet mouth. His hands moved downward and her underwear soon lay on the floor.

Larry started kissing every inch of Shae. His head went lower and lower. It seemed to take forever for his lips to find the center of her. When he did, he hesitated. He'd never gone down on a woman before, but he wanted his first experience to be with the woman that he loved. He breathed in deeply as he took the small, delicate part into his mouth. As he sucked, he could taste her juices, which he swallowed hungrily. He blew on her bud and experienced her reaction. Her moans had him throbbing with arousal. He stuck his tongue inside the opening and she froze.

"Don't," she protested in a weak voice. The things Larry were doing to her felt so good- better than the vibrator had ever felt. His mouth was so hot and his tongue so wet. She really wanted him to go on forever, but she had to stop it before it got out of control.

"Shae, don't start tripping," he said huskily. "You let me go this far. Why are you stopping me now?" He brought his head up from between her thighs and looked at her.

"I just don't want to. You know I ain't never did this before. Let's just stop. Okay?" She pleaded half-heartedly, and tried to sit up. She remembered that she'd promised never to give herself to anyone from the projects. Technically, Larry wasn't from the projects, so he didn't really count.

"But, you *do* want to do this," Larry stated. "I can feel it." He pulled her against him and drowned her with heated kisses. An image of her with Dana flashed across his mind. He wouldn't let some drug dealer get with *his* girl first. He would make sure of that. "Come on, Shae, let's lose our virginity together."

When she offered no further protest, he positioned himself between her thighs and pushed into her softness. She cried out from the slight pain and discomfort, but he stifled the sound by kissing her. He stroked in and out until he felt her loosened up.

Soon Shae raised her hips to meet him. Her body seemed to react on its own. Suddenly, she wanted Larry to go deeper. She pulled at his butt, allowing him to sink further into her love nest. She found herself wrapping her legs around his waist for even deeper penetration.

"You feel so good," Larry moaned, as his thrusts became more powerful. He tried to hold back until she'd gotten satisfaction, but he felt himself slip. "Oh God, Shae." He pushed into her as deep as he could go. She dug her fingernails into his back and bit down on his shoulder as she reached an intense orgasm. He could feel her muscles gripping him, and it drove him wild. He erupted like a volcano, spilling his lava deep into her crevices. "I love you," he whispered. He doubted she'd heard the confession.

Once it was over, they lay still, side by side in the double bed. Larry took Shae's hand in his and kissed the palm of it. Then he kissed each of her fingers.

"You okay?" he asked, after a while.

"Yes," she whispered. Her head still reeled from the mind-blowing experience.

"I didn't hurt you, did I?" His soft eyes were questioning and filled with love.

"I'm fine," she assured.

"Look," he said. "I didn't mean for this to happen. I-"

"Forget it, Larry. It's okay." She squeezed his hand.

"Are you sure?"

"Yes, I'm sure. I'm glad you were my first. You're special," she said. She gave him a hug then smiled.

"You mean that?" He'd been waiting to hear those words for ten years. It warmed his heart.

"Yes, I mean it. Now, get dressed. My mama could come home any minute," she warned.

"Oh shit." Larry scrambled off the bed and began searching for his clothes. He pulled them on in record time.

Shae laughed. "You broke the world record getting dressed," she giggled.

"Hurry up, Shae. I don't want ya moms catching us. How would I explain?"

"Chill out, Larry. I was just joking. My mom is out drinking somewhere."

"Oh." He relaxed and sat down on the edge of the bed. "What about ya grandma?" he asked.

"She can't walk up the stairs because of arthritis and her bad hip," she told him.

"Oh? In that case." He reached for her again.

"Stop. We can't do it anymore. I don't want to get pregnant," she reminded. "Wait until I get on the pill. I know you don't have a condom."

"It's a little too late for that, you think?" He glanced down at himself. "I mean, we did just do it with no protection."

"I know. But, we'll be careful the next time."

"You mean you'll let me do it again?" His eyes widened. "For real?"

"I'll think about it." She got up, went over to her dresser, and pulled some clothes out of the drawer. "Were you really a virgin?" she asked.

"Yeah," he answered, averting his eyes. "Of all questions, why you had to ask that one?" he stated dryly.

"I just find it hard to believe," she told him.

"Why?"

60

"You seemed to know what you were doing to me," she said.

"Oh, I learned that from watching porn flicks," he admitted and smiled self-consciously. "Let's keep that between me and you, though. You know, the part about me being a virgin. My dawgs would have a field day with that info."

"You have nothing to worry about. I won't tell a soul," she promised.

He stared at her with a doubtful expression. "Not even your cousin, Tashae?"

"She'd be the last person I'd tell. She talks too much."

"I know," he said dryly.

"Get off my cousin, now."

Heart swelling with pride, he watched as Shae brushed her hair. She was so beautiful and out of his league. He felt like he was floating on cloud nine.

"I can't believe we actually *did* it," Larry said after a while. "And you let me be the first guy. Man, I must be one lucky motherfucker."

"Must be," Shae replied. "I'll be back." She put the brush down and went to take a shower. Larry fell back on the bed, chuckling in glee.

"As my aunt would say—God is good all the time."

After Shae showered and dressed, she and Larry sat around listening to CD's and talking. They kept giving each other meaningful glances, but didn't mention what happened earlier.

"Shae? Shae, you up there?" Ma Violet's voice rang out, but the music drowned out her words.

"Can you that down? I think Ma Violet is calling me." Larry lowered the stereo's volume.

"Shae. Gal, is you up there or not?" They heard.

"I thought I heard her." Shae jumped up and went to the door, opening it. "Yes, I'm here. What is it, Ma Violet?" she asked.

"Some guy here for you."

"Who is it?"

"I don't know. I ain't never seen him befo'. He mighty handsome," she added.

"I wonder who that can be," she said. She didn't notice Larry's face tighten.

"Well, why don't you just run down there and find out?" he said. She glanced his way.

"What's your problem?" She didn't wait for an answer. She didn't have time for Larry's show of jealousy. After all, he wasn't her man. Just because he'd popped her cherry didn't give him the right to control her. Ignoring him, she walked out the door and hurried down the stairs.

Larry lingered behind. He wondered how Shae could even think about anyone else after what they'd just shared. He'd been looking forward to spending some quality time with her. He'd been working up the nerve to ask her if she'd be his lady.

Obviously, he'd misread the signals. Shae didn't feel the same way about him that he felt for her. Having sex with him hadn't meant anything to her. He was just another scheme in her games, and he felt played. The last thing he wanted was to pave the way for the next man. If Shae hooked up with that drug dealer, he'd be so disappointed. Hell, he'd be pissed off.

His jaw clenched and unclenched. Before following Shae, he took a few quick breaths and counted to ten. Once he'd regained control, he went downstairs.

"You still here?" Ma Violet asked when he stepped into the living room. "I thought you was gone." She struggled to balance the walker and lower her body into the rocker at the same time. Larry hurried over to assist her. "Thank you, baby."

"Yeah, I'm still here," he said. He pushed the walker to the side. He watched as she made herself as comfortable as possible. "Not that anybody noticed," he added, adjusting the pillow behind her back. Ma Violet smiled in gratitude.

"That hot tail girl of yourin out there talking to some hoodlum," Ma Violet said. She spread a colorful throw over her lap. "Look like a drug dealer to me with all that gold 'round his neck. He even got it in his mouth. Lord, have mercy." When she said those words, Larry immediately went to the window and peered out. He groaned aloud when he saw Dana. "Pretty tough competition, huh?" Ma Violet was never one to bite her tongue.

"Not really," Larry denied. "Once Shae wakes up, she'll realize that I'm the only man for her."

"Humph." Ma Violet began rocking. "She might sleep longer than Rip Van Winkle. You think you can wait that long?" She fixed him with a keen stare.

"She'll be mine," he said with determination. "I'll wait until eternity if I have to."

Another "humph" came from Ma Violet, but she said nothing further. Larry walked out of the apartment with a set look on his face. He didn't bother to speak to Dana.

"See you around," he growled.

"You don't have to le-" Shae began, but Larry's glare silenced her.

"Yes, I do. See you," he said again, and walked off.

"That's ya man?" Dana asked as his eyes bore into Larry's back.

"No. He's just a friend," she replied.

"Is he a friend with benefits? He didn't look too happy."

His eyes narrowed in distrust. That nigga hadn't shown him an ounce of respect, not even a nod. Something had to be up between them and he'd get to the bottom of it. Besides, he knew that most women lied with straight faces. Conniving ass bitches.

His eyes narrowed as he stared at Shae. If he were dealing with a trifling ass ho, it wouldn't be too long before he found out.

"You sure y'all just friends?

"Yeah," Shae told him. "We grew up together. He's like a brother to me," she lied. She smiled her most winning smile at Dana and could immediately see his reaction. He forgot all about Larry as he gazed at her.

"Do you want to go for a ride?" he asked. He wanted to feel her out and get inside her head. It really wasn't hard to figure most hood bitches out after spending some time conversing with them. He'd know just what category Shae fit in soon enough.

"Yeah. Let me get my keys, and I'll be right back."

Shae went inside and asked her grandmother if she would cook supper. It surprised her when Ma Violet agreed without argument. Shae hurried back outside, not wanting to keep Dana waiting too long.

"Where we headed?" she asked.

"Wherever you want to go." He flashed a gold plated grin. "You're pretty," he told her. She glowed from the compliment. It wasn't as if she didn't already know, but hearing it from him made it special.

They walked through the projects in order to reach his car. Curious eyes followed them. If they didn't know Dana, they could easily figure out what he was about by looking at his flashy ride. Most of them knew of him though. None of them would voice their opinions aloud out of fear. Diamond Dog was crazier than a rabid rooster and known to be trigger-happy.

"Why did you park so far away?" Shae asked.

"I didn't know which apartment you lived in. I just parked and knocked on a few doors until I found out." He unlocked the door and held it open for her. "The last time I saw you, you said I'd find you if I really wanted to."

"I guess you really wanted to." Shae smiled as she got into the car.

"That's right." He walked around and got in on the driver's side then turned to face her. "You don't mind if I run a lil errand, do you?"

"No," she replied. She had noted the expensive, spinning rims on his car and the paint job. "What's all this for? Make you feel like a king or something?" He started the car and smiled.

"Yep. This is my baby." He patted the steering wheel affectionately. "Wanna hear some music?" She nodded so he popped a CD into the disc player. Some song by the rapper TI blasted in her ears. "Are you hungry?" he asked. Shae started to declined but realized that she actually did feel hungry.

"Yeah."

"What you want? Chicken?" She turned up her nose. "Taco's? Hamburgers? Lobster? Skrimp?

"Skrimp?" She laughed.

"That's ghetto for shrimp," he explained. "We can get some skrimp and some Colt 45," he joked.

"Nah, that's okay. I think I'll settle for Chinese food," she replied.

"All right. But I don't eat that stuff. I'll stop by Reds Snak Shak and get a Big Red's burger or something," he told her.

"I don't have an appetite for grease at the moment," she said. She actually liked eating food from Reds Snak Shak, especially their gizzards and fried okra.

"I might swing by Church's Chicken."

"The last time I got some chicken there it tasted like they re-used some old grease. But, I like them better than KFC."

"Their extra crispy taste more like burnt," Dana said.

"I don't go to KFC anymore 'cause one of the cashiers who work there don't like me. I wouldn't put it past that heifer to spit in my food."

"That's nasty. Bitches be trippin'."

Dana took a sharp turn around a corner causing her to fall against him.

"Can you drive?" she asked sarcastically, moving back over to her side. He chuckled.

"Can you?" he asked. She'd mistakenly thought he was trying to be a smart aleck, but he looked at her in all seriousness. "Well? Can you drive?" he repeated.

"Yes. I just don't have a car, yet." A guy named Wayne taught her to drive in the Wal-Mart parking lot. He was another paymaster who tried to buy his way into her panties.

"I might let you drive my baby one day, but we need to go car shopping for you real soon." He said the words as though no explanation was necessary. He would be buying. Shae didn't know what to say so she said nothing.

Dana pulled into the driveway of a huge, two-story house. "I'll be right back." Before he could get out of the car, a guy wearing no shirt opened the front door and peered out.

"Diamond, what the fuck I done told you 'bout bringing people 'round here?" he scolded, glaring at Shae.

"Man, chill. That's my new lady. She's okay." The guy looked at Shae with suspicion written all over his face.

"Man, you make sure she is. We got too much to lose. We don't need the heat on us." He went back inside.

"Don't pay no attention to that nigga, Wade," Dana said. "He's schizophrenic. Paranoid. I'll be back." He disappeared into the house. After a few minutes, he returned. "One mo' stop and then I'll get ya food."

"Fine," she replied, her mind elsewhere. She couldn't stop thinking about what had transpired between her and Larry. She'd always dreamed that her first time would be a memorable experience. Now it would be because she and Larry had lost their virginity to each other.

Dana noticed that Shae seemed to be miles away. He didn't appreciate the fact that she wasn't giving him all of her attention. She was in *his* world, after all.

67

"You got ya mind on that nigga?" he questioned, dragging her back to the present.

"What?" she asked.

"I want you to know that you with me now. So, get ya mind off other niggas," he commanded.

Shae stared at him, wondering if he'd lost his mind. He glared back at her. There seemed to be a deep, smothering anger in his eyes and something else. She turned away and gazed out the window.

"Look at me." He grabbed her chin, snatching her face around.

"What's ya damn problem?" she asked, slapping his hand away.

"You should know from the jump that I don't like to share," he said, pointing into her face. "If I ever hear of you fucking up on me, you'll find out why they call me Dog."

"It ain't like I'm your lady," Shae snapped. "You don't own me. And get your finger out my face."

Dana's eyes darkened, but he complied even though he really wanted to shake her. The silly bitch didn't know who she was fucking with. In her world, she might be allowed to get slick at the mouth, but in his world, she was close to getting pimp slapped. His hand itched to do just that. But, he held off. He didn't want to run her away just yet. He had to get them drawers first. If he smacked her, she might not stick around to open her legs. And he *had* to have that. The talk of the projects was that she hadn't given it up to nobody. She was holding onto it like it was a prize or something.

"Think whatever you want, Shae," he said. "After today, ain't no other nigga gonna step to you. The word is out. You are mine." He ended the conversation when he turned up the music. "So,

68

what you wanna do after you finish eating?" He changed the subject, behaving as though he hadn't recently threatened her.

Shae couldn't believe his audacity. He really did think he was a king and that he could just rule whomever he wanted to. Well, he wasn't going to rule her.

"Let me out of this damn car," she said.

"Why? I thought you wanted Chinese food."

"I lost my appetite. Let me out or just take me home," she insisted, crossing her arms.

"Why you tripping? Did I scare you?" He pulled the car over to the side of the road, put it in park then stared at her. "Look. I'm sorry. I didn't mean to scare you. I just believe in being straight and keeping it real. If you gonna be my lady, I don't want you with nobody else."

"Who said that I wanted to be your lady? We just met."

"I know what I want, and I want you. I think you want me, too, or you wouldn't be sitting there." He leaned in and kissed her, catching her off guard. When she realized what was going on, she resisted. She pushed at his chest, but couldn't get him to stop. His lips weren't loving or affectionate like Larry's. In fact, his touch felt rough and demanding.

Dana straightened, put the car in gear and continued driving. Her getting stiff and acting all prudish didn't bother him. She'd loosen up in time. Just the way a good ho should. They always did. Especially once he started spending money on her. That's all hoes wanted anyway. They wanted a nigga to spend his cash and lay down the dick. Money and dick; those were the only two things that made tricks happy.

PROJECT QUEEN

He couldn't wait to test Shae out. He could tell that she was green. She was a pretty bitch, though, real damn pretty. She was what they called a dime. He'd be happy to have her on his arm, showing her off, making the other niggas hate. He'd teach her young, naïve ass a thing or two. She'd either learn to play the game or get played.

He chuckled to himself. He was determined to be the first man to hit that. She probably didn't even know how to suck a dick, yet. But, in time, that would change. When he got finished with her, she'd be better than the ones who swung around a pole or turned tricks on a regular basis. Plus, she'd know how to suck the skin off a dick. He only got down with the bad bitches and a bad ass bitch is exactly what he'd turn her into. She'd be a ride or die bitch before long, courtesy of Diamond Dog Dana.

After the brief moment in which he'd snapped at her, Shae noticed that Dana behaved like another person. He gave her his undivided attention and became witty and playful. By the time he walked her to the door once the evening ended, she'd decided that he wasn't half bad. She'd give him another chance.

"So, when will I see you again?" he asked.

"That's up to you," she said.

"Ok. When I come by I don't wanna see that nigga I saw here earlier," he warned, reverting back to his other personality. "I'll be by tomorrow."

He got in his car, and she watched as he drove away. For some reason, she wasn't disappointed that he'd left. Maybe hooking up with him wasn't such a great idea after all. He could prove to be trouble, which was the last thing she needed. But, he could also be her way out of the projects.

Tia and half of her family members sat outside eating garlic crabs. They craned their necks to check out Dana and his ride. Shae thought about cussing them out but ignored them instead. She wasn't in the mood to get into a fight and knew that would happen if she said anything.

"Ain't that Diamond Dog?"

"Yep," Tia said.

"She messin' round with a nigga like dat? It won't be long before he turn her out."

"She already a stuck up ho. Think she too good for the projects. Somebody need to turn her *too cute* ass out," Tia said.

"Like they say, if you lay down with dogs, you get fleas."

The big women cackled like hens then went back to stuffing their faces. Shae gave them a murderous look then hurried inside. She'd heard every word because the dumb heifers were too ghetto to talk low. She hoped they'd all choke on a crab claw. Jealous, out of shape, bitches.

CHAPTER FOUR

W
here the hell you been?" Mrs. Byrts started
in on Shae the moment she walked through
the front door.

"Out," Shae snapped. She was fed up with being
treated like a house slave. She had every right to go
outside if she wanted to. She was a grown ass
woman.

"You know you supposed to be watching the
kids. I can't deal with 'em and neither can ya
grandma."

"They ain't my kids. Why can't I do nothing
without you jumping down my throat?"

"You doing more than you supposed to be doing,
so you better watch ya damn mouth," Mrs. Byrts
said. "What the fuck you doing letting Larry into my
house when I ain't here?"

"Ma, Larry comes here all the time. Why you
tripping 'bout it now?"

"I guess you let him in ya room all the time, too,
huh?" Her voice dripped with sarcasm. "Did you let
that boy fuck you? Did you spread ya legs to him?"
she asked in an evil tone. Shae didn't answer. "Since
you ain't denying it, you musta gave it up. You finally
became the slut I done said you was?" Shae couldn't
believe that her mother had the audacity to ask her
about something so personal. It wasn't like she cared
anyway.

"Get off my ass. Damn. If I did sleep with him,
it's my body," Shae said. She didn't even care if she
made her mama mad. She was tired of her nosey ass
all getting in her business.

"Are you spreading ya legs to every Tom, Dick,
and Harry now? You gone been done caught
something," her mama hissed.

72

"I'm not spreading my legs to nobody, Ma. How many times I got to tell you?"

Mrs. Byrts grabbed her by the arm in a claw-like grip. Her long, sharp nails dug into Shae's skin. "I saw the blood on the sheet, tramp. So I know you let that boy pop ya cherry. Now that you finally got a taste of what a dick feels like, you'll be out in the streets trying to get it all the time. You hot in the ass just like that no good sister of yours."

"I'm not a tramp and neither was Vivian. That man forced himself on her. It wasn't like she wanted to have sex with him." For years, Shae knew the truth, but Vivian swore her to secrecy. She saw no reason to hold it in any longer. Maybe her mama would finally shut up about it. "Vivian got raped and it was your fault." She snatched her arm away from her mother's painful grip. Her nerves had stretched to the breaking point.

"What is you saying, girl? Nobody raped my daughter. I know better."

"Yes, someone did. I saw it happen. Vivian tried to fight him, but he held her down and took what he wanted." Shae stared at her mother with eyes filled with fury. "It was your drunk boyfriend, Percy, who did it," she spat. "He came into our room all the time and he used to feel on me, too. That's why I didn't like him and I didn't trust him. You let a child molester live with us."

For a second, Mrs. Byrts stood motionless. Her eyes narrowed. Then, she hauled off and delivered a backhanded slap that made Shae's head reel.

"You lying heifer. I don't associate with no pedophiles, let alone let them live in my house. You best be keeping that to ya self," she warned.

73

"What's going on?" Ma Violet cut in. "Bertha, what you hittin' that chile fuh? What'd she do now? I didn't see her do nothin'."

"Mama, stay out of this."

"Excuse ya self, Missy. Remember that I'm ya mama," Ma Violet said. "Let that chile alone. I ain't gonna sit here and let you beat on her- on none of 'em."

"This lying lil bitch is gonna get her tongue snatched out her mouth."

"Wait a minute now. That foul language gots to go. Bertha, don't make me go up side ya head with this here cane. Now, I don't condone abuse and I will not tolerate ya disrespect." Ma Violet had risen out of her rocker in her anger. She stood glaring at her daughter.

"Mama, you can't tell me how to run my house. This is my house," Mrs. Byrts bellowed.

"I don't care whose durn house it is. I say you ain't gonna beat on these chil'en no mo' and I means what I say. Now, I'm tired of it. You go on out there and carry on in the streets any kinda way. But, you ain't gonna do it up in here. You ain't gonna beat and whup on these chil'en. As long as I have breath left in my body, I'll see to it that you don't." Ma Violet, nostrils flaring, stared her daughter down. It was obvious she meant every word.

Mrs. Byrts gave her mama an evil look but said nothing further. She turned and stomped off to the kitchen. She opened and slammed the cabinet doors. They could here her pouring herself a drink.

"Baby, you alright?" Ma Violet asked.

"Yeah." Shae felt like bursting into tears. She wanted to tell Ma Violet everything but couldn't. She felt the heat from her mother's gaze burning into her.

Her tongue stuck to the roof of her mouth. She saw her mama giving her the evil eye as she stood drinking her liquor. Not even Ma Violet could save her from the devil. "I'm going to my room," she finally managed to get out and hurried up the stairs. Once safely behind the door, she threw herself across the bed and cried until her head pounded.

She's driving me crazy, she thought. *I've got to get away from here.*

Her mother was a dried-up, bitter woman with the blackest of hearts. She cared about no one but herself.

As Shae lay there, scenes from the past flashed through her head. She remembered the time her mother smashed Vivian's face into a closet mirror. Vivian had to get thirteen stitches and to that day, she probably still had the scars.

The kitten incident still caused her to have nightmares. In a fit of rage, their mother had stomped the animal to death before their horrified eyes. That poor cat had been helpless, and they hadn't been able to save it.

Mrs. Byrts was a mean, evil-hearted woman, especially when she drank. She could be ruthless. Shae hated living under the same roof with her and would move the first chance she got. Even though she worried about her brothers, she had to get out. If she didn't make a break, she feared what would happen.

Shae thought about her oldest sister, like she'd done so many times in the past. Vivian had left long ago and she hadn't looked back. Shae couldn't do the same. She didn't want to leave her younger brothers behind. Who would stand up for them when their mama went berserk? They needed her to protect them.

She vividly remembered the last time she saw Vivian. Mrs. Byrts kept pounding Vivian's head into the wall. Even when the blood had run down her face, the woman kept hitting her with closed fists. Once the beating ended, Vivian laid battered and bruised, curled in a fetal position.

Shae cleaned up as much of her sister's blood as she could. When she tried to help Vivian up, Mrs. Byrts tossed her across the room for her efforts. Shae scrambled under a table where she stayed hidden until the angry woman finally left.

Later that night, Vivian packed most of her clothes and split. No one in the family had seen nor heard from her since. She hadn't even sent a postcard.

Shae got up. Ignoring the spinning of her head, she went back downstairs. She fixed the twins a sandwich then helped them get ready for bed. As she ran water to wash the dishes left in the sink by her mother, Mrs. Byrts sat in front of the television eating Häagen Dazs ice cream. She ate straight from the carton with a large tablespoon.

A hatred that Shae had never felt before swelled inside her chest. She wanted to bash something heavy over her mother's head and watch the blood gush out. Just like her mother pounded Vivian's face in, Shae wanted to do the same to her. She gripped the edge of the counter.

"Shae, you lettin' the water in the sink over run, baby," Ma Violet told her, but Shae didn't hear. Something dark and sinister had cut off her air supply and she couldn't breathe.

She whirled around and ran for the front door. She needed to get away before she suffocated or went completely insane. She ran in no particular direction. Her feet refused to slow down even though her lungs protested. It felt as though she was escaping hell and she never wanted to return.

Strong hands grabbed her and she fought desperately to break free. She didn't want to go home, ever. She didn't want to live with her evil mother another day. No one could make her go back there. The hands on her might try to force her to go back. She struggled harder with the person who held her.

"Shae, what's wrong with you, girl? Stop fighting. Hey, it's me. Shae." She opened her eyes and stared into Larry's familiar face. She let out a huge sigh of relief, stopped struggling, and rested her head against his chest. "Are you okay? What you doing running around here at night? Is somebody chasing you?" She shook her head. "Are you okay?" he asked again.

"No," she whispered. He encircled her protectively in his arms.

"What's wrong? Did that drug dealer do something to you?" His face tightened at the thought.

"No, Larry. Stop jumping to conclusions. It's got nothing to do with him," she finally said.

"Then talk to me. Tell me something." He took her hands in his. "You had such a strange look on your face. I called you about five times, but you didn't hear me. You kept running, so I followed. Tell me what's bothering you."

"It's my mama," she finally admitted. "I- I hate her."

"Nah girl. Don't talk like that."

"You said you wanted me to talk to you, so I am."
She pulled away from his embrace. "You gonna listen
or not?" She stared at him. Sensing the seriousness
of the situation, he remained silent. She continued.
"My mama used to beat the hell out of my oldest
sister Vivian. One day she beat her so bad that Viv
lost consciousness. Mama just kept on beating her.
The only thing that stopped Mama from killing her
was that Toby had one of his asthma attacks." She
let out a shaky breath and went on. "Vivian got
pregnant when she was fifteen-years-old. Mama beat
her until she lost the baby.

"She would have bled to death if I hadn't run
next door and begged the neighbor to call an
ambulance. I was so scared to go back home 'cause I
knew I would get it. But, I had to do something."
Larry grabbed her hand again and squeezed it for
support. "Anyway, when I finally went home, Mama
broke my arm. That happened when I was eleven."

"Shae stop." Larry managed to breathe. He
remembered that time when Shae had worn a cast.
They had both been in the fifth grade. He'd been the
first one to sign it. He'd always thought she'd fallen
off her bicycle; that had been her story back then.

His eyes filled with tears upon learning the real
reason her arm had been in a cast. "I just can't listen
to no more," he pleaded, but she continued anyway,
needing to get it all out.

She told him about the time Toby had brought
home the stray kitten. It had been an orange and
white mutt, but they hadn't cared. Their mom had
been upset because GTE had disconnected their
phone service due to non-payment. She tripped over
the kitten on her way to the kitchen. When she
returned, Toby had the small animal cradled in his

arms. She snatched the kitten and slung it to the floor. She proceeded to stomp the cat until it became a bloody mess upon the tile. Then she sat down with a bowl or collard greens and ate them as though nothing had taken place. She had the nerve to tell Shae to get her some hot sauce.

Shae remembered how she had to scrape up the smashed cat. She fought the urge to vomit until she made it to the dumpster outside. Then, she hurled her guts out. She threw up so much that it hurt, leaving her stomach muscles sore for days.

"Shae." Larry grabbed her by the upper arms. "Please. I don't want to hear no more. This is some crucial shit. I can't listen to no more." Tears streamed down his face, but he felt no shame. He pulled her to him and held her so tightly that she could barely breathe.

"I was running 'cause I needed to get away," she said. "It felt like I was suffocating. I wanted to do terrible things to my mama. I felt hatred, a real, deep hatred for her."

"Look." Larry bit the corner of his lip and held the sides of his head as he thought. "You don't have to go back there," he finally said. "Come home with me. My aunt, she's real nice. She's old, but she's real nice. She'll let you stay with us." His grip tightened. "Shae, please get out of that place. I had no idea... Damn." Her confession had him bewildered. All those years she'd kept it a secret. Now he knew the reason that she and Toby had worn long-sleeve shirts most of the time, even during summer. They were covering up the signs of abuse. It explained why their oldest sister had left home at such a young age. No one had ever guessed, not even close friends. The years of pain that they'd endured all alone made Larry feel

79

PROJECT QUEEN

nauseous. He couldn't get the picture of the
murdered cat out of his head.

"Larry, I will leave. But, not yet." She sighed. "It
won't be long though," she said more to herself than
to him. She saw Dana as her way out.

"Shae, don't go back," Larry pleaded. "Come
home with me," he coaxed. "At least stay for the
night. Please."

She found herself being led by him and offered
no resistance. Suddenly, she felt so tired and
drained. All of the strength seemed to seep from her
body.

Larry lived right across the street from the
projects in a small, neat, pink house. Shae could still
see the neatly trimmed hedges and mowed lawn even
in the darkness. She'd never been inside Larry's
home before. She hadn't been allowed. Finding out
that she'd gone inside another kid's house would
definitely have caused Mrs. Byrts to go berserk.
She'd told them to never take their asses inside
anybody's house. Their friends weren't allowed inside
their home either.

"You sure your aunt won't mind?" she asked.

"I'm positive. Come on." He tried the knob only to
find the door locked. "She must have stepped out for
a while," he mumbled as he reached in his pocket for
a key. His aunt never locked her door even though
the neighborhood was considered unsafe. She held
firmly to the belief that God would always protect her
and her home. She'd told him often to read the book
of Psalm and to ask God for protection. She said she
never feared anything because each day she put on
the whole armor of God. Larry didn't know exactly
what that meant because he didn't read the Bible
that often. But, he did know that no one had ever

80

tried to break in all the years he'd lived there. He guessed his aunt's faith must work.

Sweet smells emanated from the house when he opened the door. It smelled like his aunt had recently baked something sweet and chocolate. They stepped inside and Larry hit the light switch, flooding the room with brightness.

Shae glanced around the living room as Larry headed for the kitchen. It was a little cluttered like most elderly people's homes she'd visited. For some reason, old people liked to keep a lot of stuff crammed into one room. Ma Violet had been somewhat of a packrat from what Shae could remember. Larry's aunt was no exception. At least all of her stuff seemed to fit together. There were no mix-matched couches or chairs. The colors were all solid, but colorful pillows and rugs gave the room a cozy appearance.

"Shae, do you want some hot chocolate?" Larry called from the other room.

"Yeah," she answered.

Shae's eyes settled on a photo of a gorgeous woman. She walked over and stared at the picture. It resembled one of those Glamour Shots. The lady wore a furry, white shawl and a string of pearls. A gigantic smile spread across her face and her eyes held a twinkle.

"That's my mama." Larry's voice startled her. He'd come up behind her with silent steps.

"She's beautiful," Shae commented.

"Yeah, well, she's dead," he answered simply. He walked into the living room and turned on the television, bringing the subject to an abrupt end.

His mother's death was the reason he'd moved from Philadelphia. It was still painful, though it had been more than ten years. He didn't want to bring up his past because Shae's situation seemed more important. Besides, his mother was gone, and he could do nothing about that. As a seven-year-old, he'd cried and prayed, asking God to bring her back. But, as he grew older, reality sunk in. She would never come back. His mother had overdosed on heroin and was dead and buried. He'd never see her alive again. Even when she'd been living, she no longer resembled the beautiful woman in the portrait. Heavy drug usage had turned her into mere skin and bones.

Larry shook his head. He didn't want to remember the last painful days of living with his mother. He'd been there when they came to remove her cold, stiff body from the bedroom. He'd never forget those vacant eyes that stared at him, haunting him for the rest of his life.

For years, it ate away at him. He'd felt so guilty because he hadn't been able to help her. Maybe trying to raise him alone had been too much of a struggle. She'd turned to drugs to numb herself from the constant reminder of what her life had become. He didn't know. The reasons were buried along with her.

Shae took a seat on the couch next to him. "Larry?" She could tell by his face that something bothered him. He seemed deeply grieved, and it tugged at her heart. "Larry, are you okay?" she asked, touching him gently on the shoulder.

"Oh." He snapped back to the present. "Yeah, I'm fine." He ran his hand over his face. "My aunt went out of town for a couple of days. Church business," he relayed. He'd read the note that had been left on the refrigerator. "You ready for that cocoa?" He gazed at her, and she nodded. He got up and she did the same, following him into the kitchen. "You like marshmallows?" he asked as he poured steaming hot water into two big mugs. He added a packet of cocoa.

"Yeah."

He placed three marshmallows into her cup and a handful into his own. He smiled mischievously at her as he did so.

"When I was a lil jit, I couldn't have but two marshmallows. But, I'm a grown man now. I can have all the marshmallows I want," he joked, bouncing back to his old self.

"So?" They both took a seat at the kitchen table. "Are you going to stay? I mean, since my aunt ain't here, you don't have to feel uncomfortable," he added.

"I- I guess I'll stay. It ain't like nobody will be worried or nothing." She took a sip of the hot drink. It should have soothed her insides, but it didn't.

"I didn't know you had it so bad," Larry said. "All those years and you never said a word. Why didn't you say something? You could have told me. I mean- I'm your best friend. It's just so much to deal with by yourself."

"I've put up with it this long. I ain't crazy yet." She tried to joke about it, but suddenly felt like crying.

"Shae." His eyes held such concern.

"I'm okay." She took another swallow of cocoa, trying to wash away the pain. It didn't work.

"I guess it's best to talk about something else." He picked up his own mug. "A week after school's out, I'm leaving for Ohio."

"I know," she said.

"James, he leaves for basic training the day after tomorrow."

"I know," she repeated.

"Well, I guess since you know everything, I have nothing left to talk about." His attempt at lightening the mood failed, so he grew silent. They finished drinking their cocoa then sat staring at each other.

The pendulum clock on the wall ticked back and forth. The silence between them grew. Larry decided to throw caution to the wind and tell Shae exactly how he felt about her.

"About this afternoon," he blurted out. "You regret what we did?"

Shae looked at him for quite a while. "No," she finally answered. "What about you?"

"Never," he said quickly. "It still feels like a dream or something," he admitted.

"It's about the only real thing that's happened in my life. I'll never regret it," she told him.

"Would you do it again?" he asked and fixed her with an intense gaze. "Right now?" She stared back and saw the love in his eyes that he'd tried, unsuccessfully, to hide. It amazed her that he loved *her*. She wasn't anyone special, just a project queen.

She didn't answer. Instead, she got up and went over to him. She leaned over and kissed him on the lips. The kiss was long and sweet. It reached down to his soul and stirred the very essence of him.

"Shae, can I make love to you?" he whispered. She nodded, so he stood. She wrapped her arms around his neck and kissed him again. Larry swooped her up into his arms and carried her to his bedroom. Placing her on the bed, he took off his shirt. He then aligned his body with hers. "Are you sure about this?" he asked, looking into her glazed eyes.

"Yes." She pulled his face to hers, kissing him with passion. She let her tongue slide into his mouth. He groaned aloud as his hands roamed over her body. Needing to feel her skin pressed against his, Larry quickly removed her clothing. He gazed at her nakedness with hunger, stood and removed the rest of his clothes.

She stared at him boldly. His penis stood fully erect, and she could see the head of it throbbing. For some reason, she moved to the corner of the bed and leaned toward it. Her lips felt his member jerk forward. Shae opened her mouth and received him. It seemed the most natural thing in the world to do. She bobbed up and down and licked it like a delicious lollipop. She could tell that Larry really enjoyed it, and it made her feel wicked in a sensuous way. When he got near the point of no return, she pulled back.

When she stopped, Larry bent down between her thighs. She moaned aloud when his tongue touched her clit. She rested back on the bed and spread her legs to allow him complete access. He licked, sucked, and blew on her until she writhed and pulled the sheets. Her moans of pleasure excited him.

This time, he was prepared with a condom. He didn't want anything to spoil the moment. He tore the package open and hurriedly slid on the protective glove. When he positioned himself between her legs, she was more than ready to receive him. He slid into her wetness. She rose to meet his powerful thrust and wrapped her legs around his waist. She wanted him to go deep. She needed to lose herself in him.

He began to move in and out, and she matched him stroke for stroke. Soon, sweat drenched both of them. Larry felt himself slipping. He groaned as he climaxed. Shae's head spun as she reached orgasm, one after the next. She could hear Larry moaning and saying how much he loved her. She found herself saying the words back.

After she came back down to earth, she stared at Larry. He had always been her best friend. He'd be leaving soon and she didn't know when and if she'd ever see him again. He'd been a part of her life for so long. She couldn't imagine what it would be like to live without him. She hadn't realized the depth of her feelings until that moment.

"I do love you, Larry," she revealed. His eyes widened. He gazed at her for a long time.

"You mean that, don't you?" he finally asked.

"Yes," she replied. He hugged her close to him as his eyes misted over. His dream had finally come true.

"I love you, too, Shae," he admitted. "So damn much that it hurts."

He just held her, experiencing so much joy that he could barely contain it. A tough little girl wearing pigtails and a frilly dress stole his heart one day at recess. As a woman, she still held it in her hands. There was nothing that he wouldn't do to keep her in his life.

It didn't take long before he felt himself stir again. He put on a fresh Magnum, feeling proud that he could wear the brand with confidence. This time, he made love to her slowly. He kissed the inner side of her thighs, and even sucked her toes. When he entered her, she felt a million fireworks explode inside her head. She called out his name over and over until her voice became hoarse. Exhausted and completely satisfied, they slept like two fat cats basking in the warm sun.

A dark figure stood underneath the broken streetlight and watched the pink house with the white shutters. He'd seen the pretty girl and the guy go inside an hour and a half earlier. He'd waited and he'd watched. Now, as he flicked the butt of the cigarette he'd been smoking on the ground, he realized that she wasn't coming out. At least, she wasn't leaving anytime soon.

He'd witnessed the two figures embrace, silhouetted by the light in the kitchen. He knew what was up when the guy had carried the girl from the room.

He rubbed the stubble on his chin and licked his lips. He knew that Diamond Dog wouldn't be too pleased to hear the news. But, someone had to tell him. Since he'd already gotten paid to do the job, he'd be the one. He got on his Beach Cruiser and rode off into the night.

Dana's car was parked in front of the house where he'd gone earlier that week. He, a guy named Kenny, and another man sat around a glass table and counted money. Drugs, ranging from cocaine, marijuana, speed, X-tasy, to crack scattered the counter top.

"Man, we made mo' money tonight than we eva made," one of the guys lisped. He had a big gap between his teeth, which protruded outward.

"Yo, Bucky, man, don't go getting too excited," Wade cautioned, turning from the window where he'd been standing guard. "When you go getting too happy, that's when the Green Team go kickin' in ya do' and bust ya ass." He turned back to the window. "Yo, y'all chill," he whispered a warning and hit the lights.

They could see very little from the glare of the television in the far corner. Their faces held panic as a heavy knock sounded on the door.

"Who is it?" Wade stood to the side of the door. He had drawn his revolver.

"Yo, man, open up. It's me, Sly," the voice on the other side called out.

Everyone exhaled in relief. Wade unlocked the door, which took quite a while since there were several dead bolts and chains. Finally, Sly stepped into the room. Wade immediately locked the door again.

"What's up, and it betta be good?" Wade snapped. "You know not to interrupt us at this time of night. You know what we doin'."

"Man, calm down, you might wet ya self." Sly said and the others laughed. Sly took a seat without being instructed to do so. "I came to see Dog," he said.

Dana's head snapped up. For some reason, he knew that Sly would have bad news. His eyes narrowed in anticipation.

"What's up?" he drawled.

"I did what you told me, man," Sly said, licking his lips anxiously. "I watched that chick all day. Every thing was going fine 'til she came runnin' out her place like it had caught on fire or somethin'. Then that nigga, what's his name? The brown skinned dude with the fucked up birthmark on his face? Uh- yeah, Larry, he stopped her. They talked for a while then they went to his house."

"What the fuck?" Dana exploded, spittle flying across the room and landing on Sly. "That bitch."

Sly frowned, wiped the spit off and continued. "Yo man, I didn't wanna hafta tell you this, but it happened like that. I saw 'em through the window. They was kissin' and shit." Dana seemed to get angrier as Sly spoke. "Then he picked her up and, I assume, they made for the bedroom," Sly finished. He delighted in relaying bad news because he thrived on the reactions. He could see the large veins standing out in Dana's neck. Dog had to be furious. It looked like he was about to do a number two right in his pants.

"So, what you gonna do, Dog?" Kenny asked. "I know I'd teach the ho' a lesson. Bitches these days think they can play games and shit with a nigga's heart. I ain't with that. You gotta knock a ho side the head every once in a while to keep her in line. Know what I mean, fellas?" All of the guys except Wade nodded in agreement, but no one noticed his displeasure.

"My lady knows I mean business," Bucky lisped. "After I stomped a few knots on her ass, she got right. Now she treats me like a king. She be givin' me massages and shit, rubbin' my feet, and suckin' my dick without me having to ask. That's the way it should be. You gotta have the upper hand. If you don't," he shrugged his thin shoulders. "Then she'll treat you like a bear skin rug. She'll walk all over ya soft ass." They all nodded again, exclaiming, "Um huhs" in union.

"I ain't got no lady," Wade finally spoke. "All them bitches ain't nothin' but trouble." He grabbed a hand of money off the table. "This right here is all the pussy I need." All of them laughed except Dana. A pulse throbbed in his temple, and he saw red. He could barely contain his anger, and it was giving him a headache.

Dana thought about how he'd make Shae pay for her mistake. He'd known not to trust her. She was too beautiful. She was just like his no good ass mama who had fucked over his daddy. His daddy had kept taking her back because he loved her so much. But, the slut had kept on screwing around. She'd ended up getting pregnant from somebody else. That's when his dad snapped. One night he crept into the other man's home and caught the two butt-naked in the bedroom. Without saying a word, he blew both of their brains out. He was serving two life sentences without the possibility of parole for their murders.

The first thing his dad had told him when he'd visited was, "Make the money. Don't let the money make you." The last thing he'd told him was, "Never trust a bitch as far as you can throw her." Dana could understand why his dad had flipped out.

He felt a blinding rage boiling inside his chest. Nobody fucked over Diamond Dog Dana without suffering the consequences. That bitch was supposed to be pure when he fucked her. Now he had to go behind another nigga. Some other Nigga was getting his piece of ass. Hell to the nah. He'd have to rectify the situation in only a way that would be satisfying to him.

***

Shae got up early, a little past nine o'clock. She slipped from the bed, trying not to disturb Larry. She

90

felt sticky from their lovemaking and wanted to take a shower.

Larry sighed in his sleep and turned onto his side. He slung his arm over and felt for Shae. "Shae?" Opening his eyes and seeing that she wasn't there caused his heart to drop. He felt relief when he heard water running.

Larry got up, headed for the bathroom, cracked the door, and peered in. He could hear Shae singing. She was tearing up a song by Keyshia Cole.

"Oh shit, that's the song," Larry said. Smiling, he pulled back the shower curtain.

"Larry," she gasped. "I thought you was still sleep." Soapy suds covered her entire body.

"I was. Then I started missing you," he said, bringing forth a smile from her.

"Get in," she told him. "Come on. I need you to scrub my back."

"Hey, no need to tell me twice." Larry stepped into the shower, under the streaming, warm water. "Turn around," he instructed. Shae did and he took a washcloth, lathered it with soap, and gently scrubbed her back. When he finished, she did the same to him. Soon, it turned into a game. They forgot about the shower as they touched each other intimately. Their bodies became heated. Larry lifted Shae up and he slid his organ into her hot sheath. He could immediately feel her muscles tighten around him.

"Girl, you are so wonderful." He pumped in and out of her. Shae bounced up and down and together they reached an explosive climax as the water cascaded down on them

The minute Shae entered the apartment, her mother yelled at her. "So, you think you grown now, right? Think you can come and go as you damn well please? Let me tell you something, Miss Bitch. If you come up pregnant, I'll kick the shit out you. Hear me?" Shae didn't answer. She closed her mind to anything that her mother said so her words fell on deaf ears. The slap she received brought her back to the present. "Did you hear what I said?"

"Don't be slapping me," Shae yelled back.

"I'll do what I damn well please. I can't tell y'all grown-acting children nothing no mo'. While you were in the streets, ya brother done messed up and got arrested."

"What?" The words shocked her so much that she forgot about being hit. She needed to know what happened to Toby. "He got arrested? When?"

"Yeah. The PoPo came around here early this morning. Drug the boy out the bed in his drawers. They didn't even give him time enough to put on his clothes."

"What did he do?" Shae asked, sliding a finger in the corner of her mouth and biting down on the nail.

"They said he shot somebody. Some dope fiend or other. Now, if you had ya ass home last night, you wouldn't have to ask these fucking questions. Get outta my face befo' I smack ya ass again." Shae stepped back. She actually believed that her mother was crazy. The lady switched off and on like a faulty light. She just shook her head and left the room.

She figured if she stayed busy, she wouldn't worry. Upstairs, she cleaned the twins' room. She dusted and vacuumed to take her mind off things. When she stood in the middle of the floor and stared around the neat room, the weight of Toby's arrest rested on her shoulders.

For some reason, she remembered James talking about a drug dealer named Chancey getting killed. Could the person responsible be her brother? She'd known that his dealing drugs would lead to no good. Easy money always brought trouble. But, she refused to believe that Toby could be a cold-blooded murderer. Now, he sat behind bars, probably scared and confused. She had to do something to get him out of jail.

A little after noon, her grandmother's voice floated up the stairs. "Shae, somebody's here to see you." She peered out the window. Seeing the pimped out Chevy, she knew that Dana had popped up.

Downstairs, she checked to make sure that her mother had left. She could barely leave the house because her mama wanted her there 24/7. But she had to get out today. She needed to put her plan into action. She figured that in two weeks she'd have what she needed. With Dana's money, she would be out of the projects and away from her mother for good.

"Hey baby," Dana greeted. "Let's go for a ride."

"Okay. Wait a sec." She stepped back inside. "Ma Violet, I'll be back before the twins come home from school. Okay?" Her grandmother nodded, and Shae flounced out. She wore Baby Phat gear, from the Kimora Lee Simmons clothing line. Her figure filled out the tee-shirt and jeans shorts.

"So, what did you do last night?" Dana asked casually, a little too casually. Shae failed to pick up on the dangerous undertones as she got into his car.

"I stayed home and watched TV." The lie came easily. She certainly wasn't going to tell him that she'd been making out with Larry. She tingled all over, remembering what happened the night before.

"Is that so?" Dana drawled. He got in on the driver's side and put the key in the ignition.

Lying bitch. He could tell by looking at her that she'd been fucked. Picturing her being tossed and turned, getting hit from the back by another nigga burned him up. He felt like punching the steering wheel, but held his anger in check. He'd take care of her deceitful ass in due time.

"Where we going?" she asked.

"It's a surprise," he stated, starting the car.

"I love surprises," Shae said.

"Oh you do?" *I have a one helluva surprise for you.* She gazed out the window, missing the evil look he threw her way.

Fifteen minutes later, he pulled up in front of a huge apartment complex where she could see a sparkling rectangular shaped pool. The grounds looked clean and well-maintained.

"You live here?" she questioned.

"Yeah." Dana climbed out. She noticed that he didn't come around and open the door for her. She decided not to make a big deal out of it, got out and followed him to an elevator. Even though they rode in silence, Shae didn't catch on that something was wrong.

Once they reached the second floor, Shae followed him off and they stopped at room twenty-four.

"Welcome to my castle," he said. He opened the door, ushering her inside.

Shae stepped into a room that looked like a showplace. An entertainment center with a high tech, stereo system covered half the wall. A large-screened television took up another side of the room. Next to the TV were an expensive VCR/DVD player and a PlayStation. He had every movie title from *Antz* to *Zorro*.

Her feet sank into the plush, thick carpet. An elegant ceiling fan hung from the sky. Dana lived in style and luxury.

"Impressive," she said.

She went to sit on the black, leather sofa, but Dana grabbed her elbow, halting her.

"Follow me."

Shae knew the moment of truth had arrived. She'd have to give something in order to get something. She didn't mind doing what she had to. Besides, Dana was attractive and had a nice physique. As long as he gave up some cash, she'd break him off with no problem.

She thought about how glad she was that Larry had been her first. She doubted that Dana would have been as patient and gentle as Larry. At least the hard part was over.

She followed him to the bedroom. When he opened the door and they entered, she saw black, velvet drapes adorning the windows. The king-sized bed was covered with black sheets; the pillows covered with black pillowcases.

"So, you watched TV all last night?" he asked.

"I already told-" she began.

"I know what you told me," he interrupted. "I want the truth this time." He jerked her by the arm and pulled her against him roughly. "Where was you at?"

"I- I don't know what you want me to say. I was watching TV." Her voice cracked. Did he know the truth?

"I had somebody follow you," he said, confirming her worst fears. "You still telling me you was watching TV all night?" His eyes narrowed.

"I- I went to a friend's house."

"Why didn't you tell me that in the first place?" he asked.

"I don't know." Her voice was low and meek.

"Because you lying. That's why." He swung out, catching her across the face with an open, backhanded slap. The power of the blow knocked her to the floor. "Get up," he growled. He grabbed her by the hair, pulling her to her feet before she could comply. "Didn't I tell you that I don't like to share what's mine? Now Sly tell me that he saw you with another nigga last night. Why you lied?" He shook her by the hair that he held in his hands then he slung her onto the bed. "Last night, that nigga got what's supposed to be mine. Now I'm taking it back." He slipped out of the jogging suit he wore. "Get undressed." Shae cowered on the bed. "I said, get undressed." He reached over and slapped her again.

She took off her shirt, but her trembling fingers wouldn't let her unzip the pants. Dana pushed her hands aside then snatched the zipper down. He roughly removed her shorts. He then ripped off the panties that covered her private parts, immediately straddling her. He spread her legs and pushed his sex into her.

"Ouch. Go easy," she begged.

"Did you tell that nigga to go easy last night?" He thrust into her further. It felt like she was being ripped apart as Dana forced his huge member inside

96

her. She'd never thought a man could be so huge. She could feel herself being stretched open.

"Ouch. You're hurting me," she cried, but he seemed oblivious to her words.

"I'll show you. I'm gonna do more than just hurt you," he growled. "You fucked that other nigga, huh?" He wrapped his hands around her throat and squeezed. Just when she thought she'd pass out from lack of oxygen, he finally released her. He then slapped her upside the head a few times. "You fucked that other nigga when I told you what I'd do if I found out. You didn't believe me, huh? You think it's a game? You think it's a motherfucking game? Bitch, you belong to me," he growled and began thrusting deeper into her. She cried out in pain but that didn't stop him from pumping and grinding inside her. When she pushed against his chest and pounded on his shoulders, he grabbed her by the throat, choking her again. She finally stopped resisting and let him have his way. The silent tears slipped down her cheeks. It seemed to go on and on forever. After what felt like an eternity, he groaned and laid still. Shae curled in the fetal position, whimpering.

"Shut the fuck up and go take a shower," he ordered.

Shae scrambled from the bed, grabbed her clothes off the floor, and headed to the bathroom.

Once she shut the door, her legs shook so badly that she slipped to the floor. She felt stickiness between her thighs and wanted to die. She could smell the scent of Dana and gagged. She couldn't believe what had happened to her. Not her. She had just got choked, slapped around and raped by a drug dealer. If she told anyone, would they believe her?

97

Would it even be considered rape since she knew Dana, and he was her boyfriend?

"I don't hear no water running," Dana yelled through the door, causing her to jump. "Hurry up. Shit, I got things to do."

She forced herself to get up and turn on the hot water. She didn't want to anger him any further, so she showered in a hurry. She winced each time she touched a sore spot. The crimson blood on the washcloth was proof that she'd never forget what happened.

Rage consumed her. Who the hell did Dana think he was, anyway? He wouldn't get off free with what he'd done. In time, she'd think of a way to make him pay. No man would use her like that and not have to suffer.

She dressed with an unnatural calmness. When she emerged from the bathroom, she found Dana in the kitchen. He had the nerve to look guilty.

"I didn't mean to lose it like that." She guessed it was his offer of an apology. "But you asked for it." He grabbed her by the upper arm and forced her face close to his. "Shae, don't ever do that again, or I might really hurt you." His hot breath caressed her cheek. "I don't want to ever see you with that nigga no more. I'll kill him and you too. You got that?" His eyes slanted. She nodded, feeling the hatred for him rise up in her throat, nearly choking her. Certain that he'd gotten his point across, he let go of her. "Come on. I'll take you home. I have business to tend to."

She followed him from his apartment, walking slowly. It felt like her entire body ached from his assault. Because of her skin complexion, she'd have noticeable bruises everywhere. She wondered how she'd be able to explain them.

Dana pulled up in front of her place. She had been quiet on the ride back, contemplating ways to kill or maim him. If he could have read her thoughts, he'd have pulled the car over and made her get out and walk.

"Buy yaself something nice," he said, slipping her a wad of bills. She wanted to spit in his face, but took the money instead. "I'll see you later. And remember what I told you about that other nigga." Shae didn't say anything. She just got out the car and waved as he pulled off.

She didn't look to see how much he'd given her until she was in her room. She counted over five hundred dollars. With that amount of money, she could bail her brother out of jail. She knew that Toby hadn't done something stupid like shoot a junkie. He didn't deserve to be locked up. He was probably going out of his mind. If she could find a ride to the jailhouse, she'd have him out before nightfall.

She went next door to use the neighbor's phone. She called her aunt Vernadine to ask if she could borrow her car. Of course, she had to fill her aunt in on everything before she agreed. Aunt Vernadine was nosey and couldn't keep a secret to save her own life. She was like the Yellow Pages. Everybody went to her for information. Shae knew that Toby's business would be all in the streets before long.

After using the phone, she went back home.

"Ma Violet, I have to go to the jailhouse to get Toby. Can you watch the twins until I get back?" Ma Violet just nodded. The twins played with their Hot Wheels in the middle of the living room floor.

"Charles and Chris, be good and mind Ma Violet, okay?"

"Okay," Both boys said, too preoccupied with the cars to even look up.

"I'll be back as soon as I can."

"Take ya time, Sugarfoot," Ma Violet said, rocking in her chair. Shae paused momentarily. Ma Violet hadn't called her that since she'd been a little girl. She could remember skipping down the aisles of the grocery store holding Ma Violet's hand.

"Sugarfoot, do you like that pretty doll over yonder?" Of course, Shae would always answer, "yes."

"Sugarfoot, I think I'll get these pretty bows for ya hair."

She'd look up at her grandmother and nod her happiness. Ma Violet would touch her on the tip of her nose and she'd giggle. The memories brought a smile to her face.

She walked the couple of blocks to Aunt Vernadine's house to get the car.

"Tell Toby to put some gas in my tank, 'cause I know he got money," Aunt Vernadine said.

"I'll tell him."

"And bring my car back in one piece. Drive carefully 'cause I ain't got no insurance," she said.

Shae just shook her head and got in the car. Black folk were always riding dirty and had the nerve to wonder why the police harassed them all the time.

She stopped by the bails bondsman. Once done there, she headed to jailhouse. It took less than half an hour to get to the police headquarters. She went inside and approached the glass partition. A balding, white guy sat behind the window. He talked on the phone, loudly. She waited until he'd hung up.

"Yes? How can I help you?" he asked once he glanced up. She told him that she'd come to pick up her brother who'd been bonded out. Once again, the man picked up the phone. After he talked for a few minutes, he hung up and told her to take a seat. "He'll be right out. They're finishing up with his release papers."

As she waited for Toby, policemen walked in and out of the building. Some stared at her with appreciation in their eyes, but she ignored them. Shae didn't like cops. In her neighborhood, they always mistreated black folk. The local black leaders were often in an uproar over the mistreatment. Demonstrations, protestations, meetings at City Hall didn't do too much to stop the violence. She'd never had an encounter with the law herself, but she knew enough people who had.

A month prior she'd witnessed two brothers getting brutalized with Taser guns. It hadn't been a pleasant experience for either of them. To make matters worse, neither had been doing anything to warrant such treatment. The cops had come out of nowhere, threw the men on the hood of a car, and begun harassing them. "They fit the description," was the excuse offered once certain groups protested.

Toby came through a set of glass doors. "Shae, I'm so glad you came to get me out," he said. "A nigga was 'bout to go crazy in this mutha."

"You wasn't even in there for six hours," she pointed out.

"Seemed like a lifetime to me." He headed for the door leading outside. He wasn't joking. It only took that short amount of time to make him realize that jail was no place for him. He didn't understand why some people treated jail like it was college, and they were career students. Thinking about how cold it had been in there made him shiver. He'd been given one thin blanket and had to sleep on a rock-hard mat. That hard shit gave him a headache.

They'd shoved two pieces of stale smelling bread with a piece of baloney stuck between them at him that morning. No mustard. No mayonnaise. Nothing. He couldn't eat that shit. He'd tried to drink the coffee but ended up spitting it out because it tasted like dirt.

He was glad he didn't have to put on that jumpsuit. Orange was not his color. Man, he was glad to be free of that bitch. They didn't really have nothing on him and since he had no priors, his bail had been reduced. He didn't know where his sister got the money to bond him out, but he was glad.

Shae got up and followed Toby. The officer behind the glass partition craned his neck to watch her.

Damn, he thought. *There ought to be a law against a woman being that fine."* He went back to shuffling papers on the desk and scowled when the phone rang again.

"So, did you do it?" Shae asked. They'd walked a distance from the building and she was sure no one would overhear. "Did you shoot that junkie?"

"Nah girl!" he denied. "I didn't shoot no damn body. I don't know what they trying to pull, but I didn't do it."

"Do you know who did?" she asked.

"Nah," he answered, but Shae caught the hesitation in his voice. She glared at him.

"Why you trying to save somebody else when you should be looking out for ya own ass?" Toby didn't answer. "You think six hours was something? Wait til ya ass have to serve ten, twenty or life."

"Look, I didn't do it, okay?" he yelled. "I can't tell on the person who did." He lowered his voice and went on. "If I tell, Shae, you, Mama, Ma Violet, and the twins will be attending my funeral. You don't go running off ya mouth to the Man. Not when you in the drug gang. You just don't do that. You don't snitch."

"Then what do you do, Toby? Huh? You tell me that. What do you do?"

He just shrugged and looked down at his feet. "Just take the rap for it, I guess," he finally said. "I'd rather do life in a cell than do time in the ground, any day."

He walked across the parking lot toward their aunt's car, and Shae followed. She didn't know what to do. She couldn't force Toby to tell on the person responsible for the shooting. Even if she could, a confession could cause him his own life.

She sighed. Life was so damn complicated. She knew the sole reason why, too. It all stemmed from their upbringing. If they could get out of the projects, they'd have a chance.

She blamed their mother. If she weren't so damn fat and lazy, they'd have a better life. Mrs. Byrts hadn't worked a full-time job since the birth of the twins. She relied on government assistant programs for help. She didn't have to pay rent because Section 8 paid it for her. She got food stamps in order to buy groceries. There was even a program that paid the electric and water. She had it made. She had a full-time babysitter to watch Charles and Chris. She never offered to pay Shae a dime when she went to her part-time job at the nursing home or hung in the streets.

Shae didn't understand why some people would want to live off the government for a majority of their lives. It didn't seem right. Capable, able-bodied people should get jobs. She definitely wanted to work but had limited resources. She hadn't thought about her future when she'd dropped out of high school. Things had been rough back then. She'd been so tired and had often failed to complete homework assignments the teachers had given. Her lack of sleep could be contributed to the constant gunfire in the projects. Not to mention the fact that she had to play mother to Toby and the twins once Vivian ran off. On top of that, she endured the constant abuse, both verbally and physically. Her energy had dissipated and she hadn't been able to carry the burdens, along with schoolwork. So, she'd dropped out when she turned sixteen.

Now she regretted her decision, but didn't know what else she could have done. She'd had to be there for her brothers because her mother refused. She felt that it was now up to her that Toby, Chris and Charles got a fair chance at life. Everything lay on her shoulders. She just didn't know how she'd pull them all out and turn their messed up lives around. But she had to do it.

As they headed home, thoughts plagued her mind. She was eighteen. She could probably get a job as a waitress, or if that couldn't happen, she'd work as a maid. Any paying job would help—McDonald's—anything. She'd find a cheap apartment and get them away from the hell they knew as the projects.

"Shae, what's that ambulance doing in front of our place?" Toby's voice alarmed her. She snapped back to the present as she put her foot on the brakes. Just as he'd said, she saw the parked ambulance. "It's Ma Violet," Toby yelled, leaping from the car before it could come to a complete stop. Shae screeched to a stop, got out, and raced after her brother.

Toby rushed over to a group of medical personnel with Shae right on his heels. "Ma Violet. What's wrong with her?" he asked one of the attendants. The man looked at him, then away. Shae stared at him, too, but he wouldn't look either of them in the eye. "What's wrong with her?" Toby demanded. "Somebody tell me."

"I'm sorry," the young attendant finally said. "We did all that we could. But—" His voice trailed off. "I'm sorry," he repeated.

"What you saying?" Toby yelled. "What you saying, man?"

"She's gone. I'm sorry," he repeated. Their grandmother's lifeless form, covered with a white sheet, lay on a stretcher that he rolled away.

The two stunned children stood on the sidewalk, too shocked to go inside.

"She was fine when I left," Shae whispered. "She was okay. Ma Violet can't be dead." She refused to believe it.

"There's nothing you kids can do," a cop on the scene told them. "Go on inside." Oblivious to his words, they both stared after the ambulance, watching the flashing lights. They listened for the wail of a siren that they'd never hear. The silence made it all so real and final.

A crowd gathered. The next-door neighbors stood outside, wearing glum expressions on their faces. For once, they kept their mouths shut. They knew how to respect the dead because it could have been either one of them. Tomorrow wasn't promised to any of them. Tia even had the decency to inform Shae that Charles and Chris were at Mrs. Watts' place.

Shae collected the twins from Mrs. Watts' apartment. The elderly woman had been kind enough to look after them once they ran over to tell her that something was wrong with Ma Violet. She went to check on her and found her unresponsive so she'd returned to dial 911.

Once the twins were in bed, Shae and Toby sat up and waited for their mother to arrive home. They'd called around trying to locate her but had been unsuccessful. Most likely, she'd gone to one of the neighborhood taverns to get drunk. She hadn't received the news about her mother's death yet.

"She should be here," Toby muttered. "Her mama is dead and she should have her fat ass here." He jumped up from the couch and paced. "I can't believe this, Shae. The one time that we need her, she ain't around. I hate that bitch."

"She'll be here soon, Toby," Shae said through the fog in her head. "Don't get so worked up for nothing."

He stopped pacing and gave her an incredulous stare. "Worked up for nothing?" he bellowed. "Ma Violet is dead, Shae. Dead. And Mama ain't here. What we supposed to do? Huh? What?" A wild look flickered in his eyes. "I'm scared, Shae," he said in a little boy's voice then the tears finally came. He could no longer hold it inside. He had about all he could take for one day. His involvement with drugs, his arrest and detainment, now his grandmother's death, it all weighed heavily on his shoulders. The only way to relieve the burden was to let it all out. So, he cried.

Shae still hadn't accepted it. It didn't completely dawn on her until that exact moment that Ma Violet was, indeed, gone. She stared at the rocker that the old woman had practically lived in for the past three months. She realized that the chair would never rock again as it held Ma Violet. She would never sit in front of the window or butt in on their conversations, either.

No matter how annoying Shae had found the old woman to be, she'd grown accustomed to having her around. She remembered talking to her late at night when the shootings and fights going on out in the streets had awakened them. Those talks were what had drawn them closer. Shae realized that she'd never really gotten to know Ma Violet, and now she'd never have the chance.

What stood out most in her mind was that only a few days ago, she'd wished her own grandmother dead. How she longed to be able to take those evil thoughts back. Why had she been granted that cruel wish? It wasn't fair.

She went over to the rocker and picked up the afghan that Ma Violet had been knitting. She'd finally finished, but she'd never have the chance to see any of them wear the beautiful shawl. Shae clutched the material close to her chest.

The ache began in the center of her soul. As she accepted the fact that her grandmother was truly gone, it spread and quickly consumed her. She tried to take a deep breath but could barely breathe. The grief smothered her, causing her chest and throat to burn fiercely.

The tears slow to come at first, rushed forth like a bursting dam. The sobs shook her entire body. She didn't feel Toby put his arms around her. She didn't feel anything except the pain in her heart.

***

Mrs. Byrts came in late that night. Shae had given up and gone to bed after midnight, but Toby fell asleep on the couch. He snapped alert and jumped up when he heard the sound of keys jingling in the lock.

"Mama, do you know?" he asked as she came into the living room and shut the door.

"Know what?" she asked. She hadn't bothered to turn on a light, so he went over and flicked the switch.

"Ma Violet died today," he stated, turning to look at her. For a split second, she appeared almost happy then her face became an expressionless mask.

"What did you say, boy?" she asked.

"She died. When me and Shae got back from the jailhouse, they was taking her away. How can she be dead?" he questioned. He hoped she'd be able to help him understand and make sense of it.

"She was old," was all she said. "It was time for her to die."

"Mama, where was you? Ma Violet is dead. What we gonna do? I mean, there's going to be a funeral, right?"

"Well, yeah."

"You gonna plan the wake and everything? She can't go out without being remembered. You'll take care of all that, right? I mean, if you need money you know I got it. I just want to know if we're going to bury her in style. You'll arrange everything, right?"

108

Mrs. Byrts grabbed the sides of her head. "Don't ask me all these questions right now, Toby," she yelled. "It's late and I'm tired. I'm going to bed." She hit the light switch on her way out of the room, leaving Toby speechless.

He sat down on the couch in the darkness, totally confused. Her mother had died, and she didn't even care. Toby couldn't figure her out. What the hell had he done to get stuck with such a psycho mama? Hatred toward her burned deep within his chest.

***

The next evening an investigator visited the apartment and revealed some shocking information. They wouldn't be allowed to bury their grandmother until an autopsy could be performed on the body.

"Why?" Shae asked. She and Toby got the news because Mrs. Byrts had left the apartment early that morning and hadn't returned.

"An autopsy is done in cases where the death is considered suspicious. Foul play is suspected concerning your grandmother," the investigator said. He wore a black suit, with a crisp, white shirt and silk tie. He carried a leather briefcase and he had a no-nonsense kind of attitude. His piercing blue eyes were narrowed in deep concentration.

"Foul play? You mean, they think somebody might have did something to Ma Violet?" Toby frowned. "Like what?"

"There's nothing further that I can tell you." His keen, observant, eyes surveyed the two children. In his mind, he wasn't questioning the death of the old woman. It was murder, plain and simple. What he had to find out was *who* murdered her and *why*.

109

From the looks of it, the two children had no clue. So, the finger had to point toward their mother.

He'd tried unsuccessfully to speak with Mrs. Byrts. She'd avoided his phone calls and hadn't shown up at her job at the nursing facility. How odd. That alone, increased his suspicion. What daughter wouldn't want to find out what happened to her mother?

He looked at the two kids again. Both seemed truly saddened by the death of their grandmother. He could tell that the young girl had been crying by her red, swollen eyes. The boy seemed to have battled with tears recently as well. He felt a sudden compassion because he'd lost his own grandmother at an early age.

It had to be the mother, who just so happened to be missing in action when he came to pay a visit. How convenient.

He softened his tone. "If anything happened to her, it will be revealed in the autopsy. You'll be informed." He took out a business card and held it out. "Could you please tell your mother it's imperative that she contacts me?" Shae took the card and nodded. "I'll be in touch. Sorry for your loss." With those final words, he left the apartment.

CHAPTER SIX

Shae, what's up?" Larry greeted. He joined her on the porch where she sat reading an *Ebony* magazine. "I haven't seen you in a while." His eyes seemed to accuse her of some unknown crime. "Where you been?"

"Nowhere really," she mumbled. The truth was she'd isolated herself while she mourned the death of her grandmother. "D-did you know that Ma Violet died last week?" she asked. Just thinking about it brought on a fresh wave of sadness. She still couldn't believe that her grandmother was truly gone forever.

"Nah, I didn't know," he said. "Why didn't you say something? I thought you'd been with that drug dealer all this time." He noticed the sadness on her face, and it tore at his heart. "I'm real sorry about that, Shae. Ma Violet, she was pretty cool."

"Yeah, well—" Her voice trailed off.

"So, will the funeral be held this Saturday?" Shae shook her head. "Next Wednesday?" he asked. Most funerals were held on those days from what he knew.

"No. They're investigating her death. Said it was suspicious. We're not going to be able to have a funeral until after an autopsy is done."

"What?" His brow furrowed as he looked at her.

Shae sighed and shook her head. "I don't know what's going on. My whole life is turning upside-down. Toby gets accused of shooting somebody, Ma Violet just died for no reason and Dana-" She stopped in mid-sentence, realizing that she'd almost blurted out her secret.

"Where does Dana fit into the picture?" Larry asked.

111

"Dana threatened me," she said, which was actually true. "He told me not to see you again. He said if I did, he'd kill both of us."

He contemplated what she'd revealed. "So, what are you gonna do?" The rumors around the 'hood pegged Dana as being a few bricks short of a wall. "I heard that Dana has some major mental issues."

"I don't know," she said. "I think he'll hurt both of us if he gets mad enough. It's true that he's not wrapped too tight. I don't want you to get hurt because of me. I'm not worth it."

"That's for me to decide, Shae," he exploded. "Girl, I love you. You know I graduate in two weeks and a week later, I'm gone. That doesn't give me a lot of time to be with you. I'm not gonna let some drug dealing motherfucker come between us. I won't." Grabbing her face between his hands, he kissed her. "I love you," he repeated. "I don't give a damn about crazy ass Dana. I can get ghetto and hood on that nigga if I have to." He tried to kiss her again.

"Stop, Larry," she protested, pulling away. "If he sees us, I don't know what'll happen."

"Why you so worried? You don't have to be scared of him. He ain't God." Just thinking about the control he already had over Shae pissed him off. Shae was supposed to belong to him, not that lowlife, money hungry, psycho piece of shit.

Shae remembered what Dana did to her the previous week and thought differently. She had every reason to be afraid, to be very afraid. How could she convince Larry to leave her alone? She didn't want him to become one of Dana's victims.

"Larry, I don't want to see you no more. Just leave me alone," she said.

"Shae, I don't buy that. Not for a second. Look me in the eye and tell me that you don't love me," he challenged.

"Larry, you know I can't do that, but you have to listen to me. It's for your own good. Just go away and don't come back. Go off to college and forgot all about me. You deserve someone who can love you freely. I'm not that person."

"Shae, there is no way I could just forgot about you." He groaned. She could tell by the set look on his face that he wasn't convinced he was in danger. He was determined to be with her. He was a man in love. The only way she could make him leave would devastate him, but it would be for the best. At least he'd still be alive, unharmed by Dana.

She spat the words out before she could change her mind. "Larry, I slept with him. I slept with Dana and...he paid me."

Larry's went rigid. Many emotions flitted across his face: disbelief, anger, and finally hurt. "Shae, that's not true. You didn't-"

"I *did*," she interrupted. "I slept with him, and he paid me. It's as simple as that."

Larry stood up mechanically. He tried to speak, but no words came out. He turned away, but not before she saw the anguish in his eyes.

He finally managed to find his voice. "How could you do that, Shae? I thought you were different. How could you?" he whispered. "After what you and me shared, I can't believe you'd stoop that low and do something so vile." His words grew stronger. "That's the type of shit a trick would do. Something one of them chicken heads would pull."

His harsh words slashed across her heart.

113

"Larry, I-" She almost took the lie back, but he cut her off.

"No," he yelled. "I don't want to hear it." He turned to face her again. Her heart constricted when she saw the disgust written on his face. "I don't want to hear shit, you feel me? Not one more word." A tear trickled down his cheek. "To think, I wanted to marry you. I was even willing to risk my life for you. But, you told me you let that nigga fuck you and it changes everything." He shook his head from side to side. "I know I shouldn't have expected you to be loyal to me, but damn. And he paid-" The words stuck in his throat. He paused. He couldn't believe she could sink to that level. But, he'd heard it directly from her mouth. He felt crushed. He couldn't do anything except stare at her. "Just tell me one thing- and be honest. Did you suck *his* dick too?"

Shae gasped. "Larry, how-"

He put his hand up, cutting off her words of protest. He wanted her to feel some of the pain he felt. He would never put his hands on her, but he could hurt her with words. "You're just a no good, slutty ass whore." With that being said, he turned and fled. He kept running and didn't look back not wanting Shae to witness his tears.

Shae stared after Larry as tears streamed down her face. She'd lost the man she loved in order to prevent him from being hurt or possibly killed. For that, she hated Dana even more than she hated him the day he'd raped her. She would make him pay. Somehow, he would pay for everything he'd done and for all the pain he'd caused.

***

The next time Dana rolled through the
neighborhood, he drove a different car. It was pimped
out like the other one. It sported spinning rims, with
shiny new hubcaps, and dual pipes. His ride made
heads turn and people pointed and talked.
Everybody knew what Dana did and what he stood
for. In the projects, he had much respect, as far as a
drug dealer could get respect.

"Shae," he called. He leaned on the horn and she
hurried outside. "Get in," he commanded. Shae
didn't have the courage to tell him no. She climbed
into the passenger's side. "Kiss me," Dana growled.
Shae leaned over and planted a kiss on his lips. He
grabbed her head and forced her lips apart. Shae sat
back in the seat. Her lips tingled from the attack.
"Here, I bought you something." Dana tossed a gift-
wrapped box at her. It fell in her lap.

"What's this?" she asked, picking it up.

"Open it." She did and discovered a jewelry set.
He'd purchased her a gold watch with tiny diamonds,
several gold bracelets, and matching earrings. "I
would have got you some rings, but I didn't know ya
ring size," he told her. "Put 'em on." After she'd
placed the jewelry on, he smiled at her. "You look
just like a queen." Shae didn't know whether to be
happy or not. She was the queen of nothing, except
for the projects.

"Thank you," she said, putting the jewelry on.
She could see Tia and her family sitting outside
gawking at them. She wished they'd just disappear.

"Them some fat ass, ugly, nappy headed hoes."
Dana said, noticing the women watching him. "You
need to move from these fucked up projects. A nigga
might get ate up by ya greedy ass neighbors. I feel

115

like a piece of steak in a pit with a bunch of starving Dobermans." Shae managed to smile.

"Oh, by the way, here are the keys to my old car." He handed her a set of keys on a key ring. "It's yours. Remind me to give you the title."

Shae's bottom lip dropped. Even though she couldn't stand Dana, she wasn't stupid. No way would she turn down a car. Besides, he owed her a lot more than that for raping her.

"Thank you." She forced herself to smile sweetly. She even managed to lean over and kiss him again.

"You be nice, I'll buy you more than that." He leered at her. She had yet to give him some head. That would happen sooner than she thought. He'd had sex with her a few more times, but she still acted all prudish and stiff. He contributed her lack of response to grieving over her grandmother's death.

He'd give her a little more time to get over it, but he couldn't wait until she loosened up and learned how to enjoy the dick. If she couldn't throw the pussy the way he liked it, what was the bitch good for? He couldn't catch a nut by just looking at her ass.

He turned on the stereo as he drove. The music blasted out of the speakers so loudly that Shae held her ears. He didn't seem to be bothered by it at all. He turned onto a notorious drug street that everyone referred to it as the "strip." When people recognized him and called out his name, he leaned up on the wheel or leaned halfway out the window and bounced in the seat. Shae thought that he looked extremely stupid, but she kept her opinion to herself. Besides, if she spoke out of turn, he just might smack her in the mouth. It was something that he did often. He didn't care where they were or who witnessed the abuse. Dana demanded respect at all costs. Shae had learned in a short amount of time to just keep her mouth shut and go with the flow.

Dana made a stop and a young man in his twenties or younger came up to the car. Shae averted her eyes and sifted through Dana's collection of CDs.

"What up?"

"You got that?"

"Yeah dawg. What it do?" Shae saw the exchange of a knot of money and a bag of what she assumed was drugs. She didn't ask any questions and feigned non-interest.

"All right Dog. One."

Dana put the money in the center compartment. "Tell that nigga Los that he got 'til noon today to come up with my shit. If he ain't got it, he know what time it is. I'll holla at ya lata." The guy nodded and Dana pulled off.

Once again, they ended up in front of the house with all the bars on the windows. The same guy from before came outside.

"Bring ya lady in, Dog," he called to Dana.

"Come on," he told her and she followed him into the house.

Drugs and money were spread out on a table. Shae stared in disbelief. She'd never seen so many drugs in one place, and it made her nervous.

"So, that's ya lady, Dog?" Kenny asked. "Damn." He stared Shae up and down until she began to feel uncomfortable. He was literally undressing her with his eyes. She took a seat and crossed her arms over her breasts.

"Man, put ya tongue back in ya mouth and wipe the foam from 'round ya lips," Wade said. They all cracked up. Shae didn't find being disrespected amusing, but she said nothing. While they counted money, put weed in tiny, plastic bags, and separated other drugs, Shae watched.

"I need to use the bathroom. Where is it?" she asked after a while. Dana pointed.

"Grab me a beer out the fridge when you come back," he ordered.

"Okay," she said, heading in the direction he'd indicated. While she was in the bathroom, she heard a lot of commotion outside. She wondered what was going on.

"Oh shit. The Green Team. The Green Team," someone yelled. Shae knew enough about drug dealing to know that if she got caught, she'd be going to jail. It wouldn't matter that she hadn't been selling any drugs and had never gotten into trouble before.

Panic filled her chest. She couldn't go to jail. No way would she be able to survive in lock down. She'd have to fight off women twice the size of Tia.

Thumps sounded at the front door, and she heard the men stampeding out the back. No one even had the decency to warn her. They just left her to her to get caught up in their mess.

She jumped off the toilet and pulled her clothes up. She didn't have time to think about wiping herself or flushing, as she lifted the window. Amazingly, it was the only window in the house that didn't have bars on it. Shae pulled herself through it and made it out just as officers crashed through the front door. She slid over the windowsill, dropped to the ground and looked around. Thick hedged trapped her, but at least they would conceal her from the police. She crawled and struggled through them. When she was finally free, she stood up and sprinted as fast as she could across someone's yard. She was too afraid to look over her shoulder. Her chest pounded until it burned, but she dared not stop.

Shae raced down Melrose Avenue, her shoes slapping on the pavement. She heard the squeal of tires behind her and knew that it was all over. She froze, preparing to throw her hands up in the air. Shit. She didn't want to go to jail.

"Shae, get in." She breathed a sigh of relief when she recognized Wade's voice. She turned around, ran over to the car, and hurried to open the door. They sped off. "Them motherfuckers came out of no where," he exclaimed. "Thank God we was on guard and got out the secret way. We're safe for now." Shae still shook visibly. "I hope you understand that we had to get out of there." She nodded as she took deep breaths to calm herself. "Anyway, that's one house they got. We gotta move on. I'm headed to my other place. Dana will be there later to get you." He continued to drive in silence. It wasn't long before he pulled up to their destination.

Wade's other place resembled a small mansion. There was a gate that he controlled with a remote. Two Rottweilers stood on guard. They barked and growled at the stranger who'd come into their territory.

"Heel, boys," Wade commanded. They immediately grew quiet and sat still. Shae stuck close to Wade's side. She stared at the dogs as they passed them. "They won't bother you unless I say so," Wade explained. The dogs didn't move, but she was glad to get safely inside. She really didn't trust dogs, especially ones with reputations for being vicious. She'd read stories about Rottweilers and Pit Bulls attacking innocent people and mauling them.

"Make ya self at home. Just chill out," Wade said, once they'd entered the house. Shae looked around the room living room. It was beautifully decorated in peach undertones, her favorite color.

"Wow," escaped her lips.

Wade watched the expression on her face and smiled. He knew exactly how she felt. He'd felt the same way when she'd walked into his house, and he saw her up close for the first time.

"If you want, I'll show you around," he offered.

"Okay." She let him lead the way since it was his place.

The rest of the house was just as impressive as the living room, but her favorite was the room with the built-in Jacuzzi. She stared at the hot tub in amazement.

"Maybe one day you can join me in that," Wade said softly. Shae gave him an innocent look. She hadn't known until then that he had an interest in her. She just smiled and said nothing. "Dana don't know how to treat a lady," Wade continued. "He's gonna hurt you. If you break away from him now- you know, before y'all get intimate- then it'll be easier on him."

Color rushed to Shae's face. "It's too late for that," she said lowly.

"Damn, man." He stared at her closely, his regret evident. "You don't look like the easy type to me." His words held disappointment.

Shae felt the need to defend her honor. She didn't want Wade to think she was some slut who gave herself to the highest bidder. She hadn't told anyone about what Dana had done and it ate away at her insides. It was a burden that she wanted to let go of. She could no longer carry it alone.

"It's not like that at all," she told him.

Wade stood about five feet eight. He had a nice physique and was fairly handsome, resembling the rapper, Ice Cube. He had light brown eyes that seemed to bore into her, reading her soul.

"What you saying? You either slept with him or you didn't."

"I didn't," she told him. "Well, I did, but-" she hesitated.

"But?"

"But I didn't want to," she finished.

"So, what are you saying?" he repeated.

"What I'm trying to say is that-well- Dana- he forced himself on me," she blurted out.

Wade stared deeply into her eyes for quite a while, and she didn't look away. It was so important that he believed her.

"Oh, I see," he finally said. "That's low. That's real low. I never thought my boy would do something like that. A real man don't force himself on a woman." He shook his head. "I'm sorry that happened to you. It was probably because of what Sly told him the other night," he added.

"What did Sly say?" Shae wanted to know.

"Dana had you watched. Sly told him that you were with some guy named Larry. I knew Dog was upset, but I didn't know he'd rape you."

"That no good bastard Sly." Shae fumed. She knew all about Sly the Crackhead. His sneaky, crooked ass, would still your drawers off the clothesline and try to sell them back to you, just for money to get a hit.

"Don't blame him. You know he's strung out on that shit. He was just doing what Dana paid him to do," Wade pointed out.

121

"I know, but he gets on my nerves with his cracked out ass." Shae sat on the couch once they returned to the living room. "I just wish it hadn't happened," she revealed. "I feel so- so dirty and used. I feel like I'll never be clean again."

"That's rough," Wade consoled. "But Dana wasn't ya first, was he? Had you been with other guys?"

"Just Larry. He was the only one," she admitted.

"Damn. I guess you feel pretty fucked up inside?" Shae nodded. "You scared of him, ain't you?" Their eyes met.

"Shouldn't I be?"

"Yeah, and that's why you need to leave that nigga alone," Wade warned.

"I wish I could, but I'm scared to leave. He said he'd kill me, and I believe him."

"I wish I could help you but Dog, he don't play. He crazy just like his daddy, Dog Chain. You his property now and I'd be digging my own grave if I put my nose in where it don't belong. I admit that I'm attracted to you. You a beautiful girl and shit, fine as hell and all that. But, I can't risk my life for you. I wish I could, but I can't. I'm sorry."

Shae sighed in frustration. No one had the nerve to go against Dana, so she'd never be free of him. She didn't have a chance with Larry now, or anyone else for that matter. She wanted to put her head in her hands and bawl like a baby. Instead, she asked Wade for something to drink. When he offered her a wine cooler, she didn't decline. She wasn't of drinking age, but she opened the bottle and downed it anyway. If she were lucky, it would wash away her sorrows. For the first time in her life, she understood why her mother drank so much.

Dana showed up several hours later. By then, she'd polished off two more of the wine coolers. Being tipsy was the only way she could look into his hateful face without spitting in it. As Dana took a seat next to her, she and Wade shared a look between them. She knew her secret would be safe with him.

CHAPTER SEVEN

A week rushed by. Dana made sure that Shae stayed with him as much as possible. He took her out to dance clubs, treated her to fancy dinners, the movies- anything that she wanted to do. On top of that, he gave her money. But as the saying goes, "Nothing comes for free." Dana made sure that she slept with him every time he gave her something. He was always brutal and had begun demanding that she perform oral sex. She hated it when he'd skeet his jism in her face or forced her to swallow it. She usually felt sick and had to throw up afterwards.

She couldn't really complain about much because it was the lifestyle she thought she wanted. She got to play the role of project queen to the hilt. She had everything she'd ever dreamed of: jewelry, clothes, money, but she still wasn't happy.

Going out with Dana did help to keep her mind off her grandmother's suspicious death. Even though she despised being with Dana, she hated being at home even more. She detested her mother. The woman seemed crazier than usual. Her temper erupted for no reason. She struck out at the twins constantly, and Shae seriously began to question her sanity.

At first, she thought her mother was acting out because of Ma Violet's death, but that was dispelled when she overheard Mrs. Byrts's conversation.

She'd gone next door to borrow some sugar from Mrs. Watts, not knowing her mother was there using the phone. Mrs. Watts sat outside trying to catch a breeze.

"Help ya self, baby," she told Shae. "I can't get these tired bones moving as fast as you can. It's in the kitchen cabinet." She said, sending Shae into the house.

Shae went inside and headed for the kitchen, but a loud voice halted her in her tracks.

"I don't give a fuck 'bout that," Mrs. Byrts said. "What the fuck y'all wanna chop her up for?" She yelled and cussed on the phone a while longer then slammed down the receiver. "I just wanna bury the old bitch and put this shit behind me." Shae heard her mutter. "Hell, people die every damn day, and they don't go 'round cutting them up. Why this gotta be any different?"

Shae ducked into the kitchen so her mother wouldn't see her. There was no telling what Mrs. Byrts would do if she thought Shae had been eavesdropping. Shae watched, unobserved, as she charged from the room and went out the front door. She breathed a sigh of relief at not being discovered.

She was confused. Why was her mama so mad because they wanted to perform the autopsy? What had she said: "*I just want to bury the old bitch.*" Why would she say something like that about her own mother?

She got the sugar she came for, thanked Mrs. Watts, and headed home. She couldn't erase the look of fury and pure evil that she'd seen on her mother's face from her mind. What was Mrs. Byrts afraid an autopsy would reveal?

From the kitchen, Shae heard the knock on the door. She thought it would be Dana so she pasted a fake smile on her face and went to answer.

"I thought you weren't-" Her words trailed off when she saw Larry standing there. He wasn't

125

smiling, and he appeared a lot thinner since she'd last seen him.

"Hi," he said. The two stared at each other awkwardly. "Can I come in?" he finally asked. She opened the door and he slid past, seeming to be extremely cautious not to touch her.

"So-" She tried to think of something to say but failed. Larry had been so upset with her the last time they'd talked. She thought she'd never see him again.

"How have you been?" he asked.

"Fine," she answered. "What about you?" she asked and immediately regretted the question. He gazed at her with so much hurt in his eyes.

"Do you even need to ask?" he said with a sad smile. "I just came to say goodbye," he told her. "I – I decided to leave a lil early to make sure things are in order," he explained, not meeting her eyes. "You know how it is with financial aid and the living situation in the dorm and all."

"I – I wish you the best," she managed to get past the lump in her throat.

"I'll miss you, Shae." He took her hand and placed it to his lips. "I'll miss you so much." He held his arms out, needing to hold her close to him one last time.

"I'll miss you, too," she whispered. She went into his outstretched arms. They stood like that for a while, just holding each other.

"You know I didn't mean what I said," he told her. "I'm so sorry for going off like that." He gently pushed her away then caressed her cheek as his eyes bore into hers. "Shae, I don't believe for one minute that you don't care." Her eyes gave away everything she felt inside. He groaned, pulled her to him again, crushing her lips with his own. "But-" he said after a while. "I know you're pushing me away because you think you have to. I can respect that. If you ever need me for anything, for any reason, don't hesitate to call. I'll be at this address. The number's right there." He handed her a card with the university's address and phone number on it. "Don't forget what we shared. I love you, no matter what," he said thickly. "Don't ever forget that." He gently wiped away the tear that slipped down her face. "Goodbye, Shae." His lips softly brushed against hers one last time.

Her heart in her throat, she couldn't even speak. She watched him walk out of her life. She wanted to call him back but couldn't. It was best that she let him go. She couldn't live with herself if Dana hurt him because of her.

"I love you, too, Larry," she finally whispered.

"Shae, I don't feel so good." Chris's weak mumble snapped her out of the daze she was in. She went over to the couch and placed the palm of her hand on his forehead.

"You don't feel hot," she said. "Lie down and rest. You too, Charles." She felt his forehead as well.

The twins had stayed home from school due to being sick. Frankly, she was beginning to worry. They had been feeling badly for the past week. Maybe she'd have to take them to the Health Department for a check up. Mrs. Byrts sure as hell wasn't going to do it. She watched as the two boys arranged themselves on opposite ends of the couch. They both looked grayish in coloring.

"Do you want some orange juice?" she asked.

"No," Chris answered and Charles just weakly shook his head.

PROJECT QUEEN

Another knock sounded on the door. It had to be Dana. Fear leapt into her heart, paralyzing her. What if he saw Larry leave the apartment? No amount of explaining would appease him.

Dana entered without waiting to be invited inside. He came over and grabbed a handful of Shae's hair. "Didn't I tell you to keep that nigga from ya house? What he doing here? Don't deny it, because I saw him leave just now." He brought his fist up and slammed it into her stomach, not giving her a chance to answer. Sinking to her knees, she cradled her belly. "What am I gonna hafta do to show you I mean business? Huh?" He backhand slapped her then jerked her by the hair, pulling her up from the floor. He threw several blows to her upper body and backhanded her again.

"Leave my sister alone," a small voice cried out. Little Charles tried to come to her aide but was so weak that he tumbled to the floor. His small body went into convulsions, causing Dana to stop his attack on Shae.

"What the hell wrong with him?" Dana asked. Shae gazed over to see her brother jerking in a fit of some sort. She forgot all about her pain as she screamed for Dana to call an ambulance. With a nonchalant look on his face, he took out his cell phone and dialed 911. "I ain't do nothing to him. So don't try to blame this shit on me," he hissed.

She ignored him and ran to the kitchen to get a spoon. She needed to keep Charles from swallowing his tongue and had read somewhere that a spoon could be used.

It seemed like an eternity before attendants rushed into the apartment. Shae had managed to keep her brother calm. The convulsions had stopped,

128

but his breathing was shallow. He appeared to be in a comatose state. She prayed to God that he wouldn't die.

The professionals soon took over. Chris cried when they placed his twin brother on a stretcher. Shae went over and cradled him in her arms.

"That little guy looks terrible. I think it's best if he came along too," one of the medics said. "He'll be evaluated and we'll find out what exactly is wrong."

Shae let him carry Chris to the ambulance. She didn't know what else to do. As usual, their mother wasn't around when needed and Toby wasn't either.

"I'll drive you to the hospital," Dana said, startling her. She hadn't realized that he'd stuck around. She nodded and they headed out.

Of course half the neighborhood had to be gathered out front. Black people were so damn nosey. Shae wanted to curse them out and ask them what the hell they were looking at. She hurried to Dana's car and got in before anyone could ask questions.

When Dana sped past the grocery store on the corner, Shae saw Toby come out.

"Stop," she yelled. "I have to tell my brother what happened." Dana pulled over. Toby came up to the car when he saw Shae waving frantically to him.

"Toby, get in," Shae said.

"Shae, I got things to do right now." He edged away from the car, staring at Dana with a strange look on his face.

"Toby, it's the twins. Something's wrong. They're on their way to the hospital." Even with that news, Toby refused to budge. He continued to back away.

"I'll be there, all right?" he said. "Just go. I'll be there." Shae didn't understand. His brothers could be dying and all he thought about was selling some damn drugs. What was wrong with him? She decided to deal with Toby later. Her main concern was for Chris and Charles.

"Just drive," she told Dana, dismissing Toby's behavior for the time being.

"After we deal with this, we got some unfinished business to take care of," Dana told her, pulling up to the hospital. He parked even though a sign indicated No Parking.

Shae ignored him, got out the car and rushed inside the building.

"My brothers, are they okay?" Shae asked the second she arrived at the front desk.

"What are their names?" Shae told her and she looked them up in the computer.

"There isn't any news on their condition as of yet," the woman said. "All I can tell you is that they've been admitted to the critical care unit on the third floor. We need for you to complete-"

"I have to see them." Shae rushed off, ignoring the clipboard of paperwork the woman extended.

Being placed in critical care couldn't be good. When she got to the twins' room, she tried to go to them, but a security guard wouldn't let her pass. "What's wrong? Why won't you let me get by? My brothers are in there."

A formidable looking doctor appeared. He heard the hysterical young woman and came out to assist the security guard. It would only be a matter of time before backup arrived because he'd already called them. He would try to keep the situation from escalating into something nasty. However, if things got out of hand, he would step to the side. He wasn't used to getting involved in brawls. The security

130

guard, a stocky black woman who resembled a man looked as though she could handle herself anyway.

"Miss, please calm down," he said.

"Calm down?" Shae turned her anger on him. "My brothers are in that room and this bull dog looking bitch won't let me go to them. How the fuck I'm supposed to calm down?"

"Miss, I'm the attending physician. I have some news, but you really have to try to control yourself," he insisted.

Shae crossed her hands over her chest and took a deep breath. She exhaled loudly. "What is it?" she asked more calmly. "Are they okay?"

"I'm afraid that your brothers have been poisoned," he replied.

"Poisoned," she exclaimed.

"Traces of arsenic were found in their bloodstreams. They are extremely sick. It's a miracle that they are still alive." His eyes assessed her as if she was the lowest form of life on earth. "No one is allowed in that room except hospital personnel. *No one*," he stressed. Both he and the security guard glared at her coldly.

It suddenly dawned on her that they thought *she* was responsible.

"Wait a minute, y'all think I did it?" Even though neither answered, their silence spoke volumes.

As the news sank in, two police officers exited the elevator and headed in her direction. "Miss Byrts?" one of them asked. She nodded as fear gripped her. The involvement of cops could only mean trouble. "Ma'am, come this way," he instructed. "We'll need to ask you some questions."

"Questions? What's going on?"

131

"We'll explain it momentarily. But for now, come with us."

"Am I being arrested? Did you call the cops on me?" she asked the doctor, who nodded smugly. "But I didn't do nothing." she stated, her voice rising with anger. She was worried about her brothers and now these police were all up in her face looking like they wanted to handcuff her. She wasn't in the mood to be treated like Rodney King. Besides, she really hadn't done anything. If she had to go to jail, it would be for a reason. She didn't feel like talking to those racist pigs. She didn't trust them and she knew how cops twisted your words and used them against you. She'd witnessed it time after time in the projects.

The elevator doors opened again and Toby came through them. She felt a surge of relief. She needed him more than ever. She took a step toward him, but the female officer restrained her.

"Stay where you are, ma'am," she warned. Shae could see her hand go to the revolver strapped around her waist.

"That's my brother," she told Trigger Finger. "He can tell you that I didn't do it." She turned to him. "Toby, they're saying that Charles and Chris were poisoned, and they think I did it," she said.

"What?" Toby looked confused. "Somebody poisoned the twins? No way."

"Yes way," the female officer retorted.
Toby tossed her an annoyed look. He didn't trust cops and the last thing he wanted to do was hold a conversation with them. However, he couldn't just leave Shae to fend for herself.

"If they got poisoned, Mama had to do it," he finally said.

132

"You think your mother is responsible?" the male cop questioned, scribbling on a yellow notepad. He was the calmer of the two. The female officer still hadn't taken her hand off her gun. She stood on edge and tense.

"Yeah," Toby nodded. "It had to be her. Shae wouldn't do nothing like that. Shae loves Chris and Charles," he said. "Mama don't." Somehow he had to make the two suspicious cops believe him. His sister couldn't go to jail for something she didn't do. She'd believed in him when he'd been falsely accused. Now it was his turn to stand by her. But, how could he make two white, biased cops, obviously used to stereotyping blacks, believe him? His best bet was to appeal to their emotions. So, he continued to talk. "Mama don't care about nothing or nobody," he said. "And, she's crazy," he added. "Let me show y'all something. She did this to me when I was twelve-years-old." He lifted up his shirt and turned around. He could hear gasps of astonishment from the female cop and the security guard. The male cop swore aloud.

Several raised scars crisscrossed half his back. His mother had whipped him with a wire clothes hanger. The horrid marks were a permanent reminder of what the cruel woman was capable of doing.

The two officers gave each other long looks, clearly affected by what the saw. The female officer sighed loudly and finally let go of her gun. She visibly relaxed and turned to the children with compassion in her eyes.

"Put your shirt down, son," she told Toby. "Come this way, please. We'll still have to question you both. It's procedure," she said quietly. Shae and Toby

133

followed them to an empty room. Shae grabbed Toby's hand and gave him a brief hug.

"You didn't have to do that," she said. She knew how painful it had to be for him. For years, they'd kept their secrets hidden. She'd told Larry and now Toby had told someone. "Thank you."

"It's gonna be okay," he promised. "Mama won't be able to hurt us no more." His eyes misted. "I just can't believe she did that to Charles and Chris, though."

"Don't worry, she'll be punished to the fullest extent of the law," the female officer said with conviction. "Come on in and have a seat. You kids want anything? A soda? Some potato chips? I'd be happy to go to the vending machine," she offered.

"No thanks." Shae's stomach was tied in knots. She doubted she'd be able to keep anything down.

"No ma'am." Toby declined as well. He didn't have an appetite. He just wanted his little brothers to live. He felt so guilty for not being around to protect them. He'd been too busy out in the streets dealing drugs. In a sense, he was no better than his mother. He'd been helping to kill his own people with a different kind of poison.

Hours later, after being questioned, they were allowed to leave. They wouldn't be permitted to visit the twins until some issues were cleared up. The attending physician agreed to talk to them, but only after the officers assured him that they were in the clear of any wrongdoing.

He updated them on their status. "Charles remains in critical condition, but Chris has upgraded to stable," he said. "We'll continue to monitor them around the clock." The doctor cleared his throat, fidgeting with a stethoscope hanging around his neck. "Earlier, I was just doing my job," he explained. Shae just rolled her eyes and walked off. When she encountered the security guard, the bitch had the audacity to look ashamed. Shae understood the white physician jumping to conclusions, but one of her own kind? Now *that* she couldn't understand.

Shae felt drained and wanted nothing more than to go to sleep. Back in the waiting room, she discovered that Dana had left. That figured. The slimy motherfucker didn't even care enough to hang around to see if her brothers had survived.

Wise for his age, Toby sized up the situation. He wasn't just street-smart: he knew things. He knew more about Dana then he was willing to tell. Of course, a big time drug dealer would dip the minute he saw cops. He'd probably been packing heat, too, and didn't want to go down on a gun charge. He hated the fact that Shae had gotten mixed up with that foul ass nigga.

"I'll take you home," he told her. "I got my dawg John's car."

"You don't even have a driver's license," she reminded him.

"Don't mean I can't drive. I been putting the pedal to the metal since I was twelve," he shocked her by saying. "Come on." She had no choice, so she followed him outside.

She felt unreal, like a mannequin. How could their mama do something so cruel? She knew that the woman had some issues, but to actually try to kill her own children? She needed to be put away.

Suddenly, it came to her as she got in the car. "She must have poisoned Ma Violet, too," she whispered to Toby. He stared at her then nodded slowly.

"She had to," he stated. As he spoke the words, he knew them to be true. He remembered how she'd reacted on the night Ma Violet had died. He thought she'd behaved strangely and now he knew why. Something else, equally important jumped out at him. "How did you get those bruises around your throat?" Toby's question jerked her mind back to the present.

"I-"

"He did it, didn't he?" he stated rather than asked. She didn't answer. "I didn't know exactly who Dana was, but now I know. That's Diamond Dog. Shae, you got ya self in a lot of trouble. He'll kill a nigga in a heartbeat. He's known for beating bitches down and stumping holes in niggas."

Somehow, that confession didn't surprise her at all. "How do you know so much about him?" she asked.

"Don't worry 'bout that. I just know. That's what's important. Stay away from that nigga. He's bad news. Trust me. Stay away from him." Her brother's voice held a trace of fear. She took a closer look at him.

"You ain't telling me everything. Why not?"

"Sometimes, it's best *not* to know," he replied.

He started the car and drove away from the hospital. About fifteen minutes later, he stopped at the curb in front of their place. "Get some stuff together. No telling what Mama might do. I don't trust her. We can stay at a hotel until we find out that she's locked up." He took control and for once Shae was glad that she didn't have to. The day had taken its toll on her. She hurried inside.

Grabbing a large Doonie and Burke carry bag, she threw some of her and Toby's clothes and

136

personal items in it and went back outside. Her heart constricted with fear when she witnessed Toby being confronted by Mrs. Byrts.

"I get pulled off my job 'bout this shit," she yelled. "I'm supposed to be responsible for poisoning my own babies? What kinda shit is that?" she asked. "They tell me that y'all told them it was me. What made you say some shit like that?"

"It was you," Toby spat. "You did it." His eyes blazed. "And you killed Ma Violet too," he accused.

"You bastard," Mrs. Byrts yelled. "I will hurt you and snatch ya lying tongue out ya mouth."

"Watch out," Shae screamed as Mrs. Byrts lunged for him. He didn't move fast enough and she caught him in a bear hug. She squeezed until he couldn't breathe.

"Shae-" he wheezed.

Anxiety overcame her. She knew that her mother would kill him if she didn't do something. Because of his asthma, his lungs were already weak. With their mother holding him, she could cut off his breathing altogether.

"Let him go," she yelled, grabbing the garden hose that lay in the front yard. She went into action. She folded it for thickness and swung as hard as she could.

When the hose cut into her back and arms, Mrs. Byrts loosened her hold on Toby. Shae hit her again and again until she released him completely. Toby escaped and ran to the car. For a moment, Shae thought he would leave her to fend for herself. Instead, he grabbed something from under the seat.

"Don't move, Mama, or I'll shoot," he yelled and aimed a 357 Magnum at her. Mrs. Byrts ambled toward him. "I said don't move," he screamed. His eyes widened with shock as his mother kept coming.

He remembered all of the beatings he'd suffered at her hands. She'd always made him feel so weak, small and afraid. So insignificant.

"You gonna shoot me like you shot that dope fiend? Well, you better make sure I'm dead," she snarled.

"Mama, please don't make me do it," he begged. He had his trembling finger on the trigger. He couldn't do it. Not him. Hadn't she always told him exactly what he was? She'd drilled it in his head for years as she'd pummeled his body with her fists. She stomped it into his memory and kicked it into his brain. He was a nothing, a no account, an idiot, a punk, chicken-hearted, worthless, pitiful, and sorry. The list seemed endless. He wondered how a mother could hate her own child so much. What had he done to deserve that kind of treatment? What had any of them done?

Vivian ran away because of their mama. Shae thought some abusive drug dealer could save her. And Charles and Chris. He almost cried when he thought about his little brothers lying in a hospital bed. They were so helpless, just six-years-old. They couldn't protect themselves. Why would she poison them, try to get rid of them like they were rats? And Ma Violet... That did it. He felt something inside of him snap.

"I ought to bust a cap in ya ass for what you did to Ma Violet and the twins," he said.

Shae stood frozen to the spot. She sensed the depth of Toby's anger and knew without a doubt that he was mad enough to do just about anything. She couldn't let it happen. As much as she despised her mother, she didn't want her death on Toby's hands. He'd never be able to carry around that type of guilt.

"Toby, don't do it," she yelled. "Run."

His fury almost blinded him. Shae's words penetrated the dark cloud in his mind. He shook his head to clear it, dropped the gun and sprinted off. Shae had already made it safely down the street. Seeing some people sitting outside, they stopped and asked if they could use their phone.

"What happened?" A woman with a tooth missing up front asked. Shae couldn't explain and Toby just shook his head still numb with shock. "Po' children seem traumatized."

"Did somebody get shot?" someone else asked.

"I dunno. Jus' hand me the cordless," the woman said.

Shae dialed 911 with trembling fingers. She could barely get the words out as she gave an account of what had taken place. The dispatcher on the other end of the phone informed her that officers would be on the scene as soon as possible. She was very sympathetic and spoke in calming tones. It helped Shae hold it together at a time when she wanted to fall apart.

Shae and Toby returned to the scene to find what resembled a swat team outside their apartment. They watched on the sidelines as policemen tried to apprehend their mother. It took five of them to restrain her.

Apparently, Mrs. Byrts had decided that she wasn't going to be taken down easily. She'd fight until the last ounce of strength left her body. It appeared that she had the strength of Samson as she battled with the officers.

One of the deputies finally got fed up with the struggle and let her have it with his blackjack. As if on cue, the other four followed suit. They went to work on her with their clubs. Even though years of hatred had built up in their hearts, Shae and Toby couldn't help feeling sorry for their mother. She had given birth to them and at one point in their lives had shown them love.

Toby ran past the blockade. "That's my mama. Don't do her like that," he yelled. Two policemen grabbed him and held him back. "Man, let me go. They gonna kill her. That's my mama." Shae ran to Toby and pulled him out of the officers' grip.

"Stop, Toby. Remember what she did," she reminded him. "She killed Ma Violet and almost killed Charles and Chris."

"I know," he finally said. "But they ain't got to beat her like that." He sobbed. "She still our mama."

Finally, the big woman lay still. The officers handcuffed her and shoved her into the back seat of a patrol car. Her head fell back against the seat. It was plain to see that she'd been beaten unconscious. Blood from an open wound dripped down the side of her face. No one cared as they got into their cars and pulled away. The deputy that had to transport her, gazed at her, spit on the ground with disgust, and closed the door. Then, he too, got in his car and sped off.

"How could she do it, Shae? How?" Toby asked. "Was it our fault?" He put his hands up to his face. He tried to be a man and not cry in front of the crowd that had gathered. For some reason them looking on like vultures made him mad. Nosey ass neighbors were always up in their business. He felt like giving them the middle finger. He could tell by the looks in their eyes that they felt sorry for them. Well, he didn't need their pity. Where the hell had they been all those years when he'd gotten his ass stomped? They all had turned a deaf ear to the abuse. Nobody had tried to help then. Now they wanted to stand around and look on like they cared. They could kiss his ass.

"So what do we do now?" he asked. "We don't know where Daddy is, or if he's even alive. Now, we don't have a mama. What do we do?" he repeated.

"Don't worry, Toby. You still have me. I'll take care of everything." She put her arms around her little brother. For the first time in her life, she felt an intense love for him. It had been there all along, but it had taken this tragedy to bring it forth. She vowed to herself that no one else would hurt her or her family again. They'd been through enough.

Toby hugged her so hard that she could barely breathe. She felt a fierce need to protect him at all cost. She'd make sure he wouldn't suffer anymore. None of them would.

After everything died down and the crowd dispersed, they went inside. Toby and Shae were too emotionally drained to think about going somewhere else that night. They decided to stay at the apartment until other arrangements could be made. Mrs. Byrts could no longer get to them since she'd been arrested.

Shae thought about Larry and wondered if he'd already left for college. At a time like this, she really could use a friend. But, it would be unfair of her to burden him with her problems. Larry worrying about her would make it hard for him to concentrate on his studies. Knowing Larry, he might even decide not to leave because she needed him. She wouldn't mess up

141

his future. She'd just have to handle everything herself.

"I'm going next door to call the hospital. I want to check on Charles and Chris," Shae told Toby. He immediately jumped up from the couch.

"I'll go with you. I don't- just don't wanna be- you know." Shae nodded because she understood. He didn't want to be alone in the apartment. They walked next door together.

Mrs. Watts met them at the door and told them how sorry she was about their mother. She'd witnessed it all and still couldn't believe it. That child had to have been possessed by some demon spirit. What else would make her carry on so? It had to be the devil. That's why she made sure that she stayed in church and stayed into God and His Word. When you strayed from that, you could easily become prey to the devil and his wiles and schemes. Satan would use anybody he could as a vessel. He's a liar and he comes to steal, to kill and to destroy. Bertha should have rebuked him in the name of Jesus. Rebuke the devil and he will flee from you.

"It's a shame, a real shame." She shook her head. "Bertha was a good kid. I knew 'em all when they was comin' up. She was a good chile. It's a shame she turned out the way she did." She ushered them into the house. "Sorry to hear about ya grandmother, too. May God bless her soul. At least now she's at peace. The Bible says, Behold, I shew you a mystery; we shall not all sleep, but we shall all be changed. In a moment, in the twinkling of an eye, at the last trump: for the trumpet shall sound, and the dead shall be raised incorruptible, and we shall be changed. Read that sometime. It's in I Corinthians. When nothing else works, you'll find that Jesus works. Always. Baby, God doesn't put more on us than we can bear. Remember that."

"Thank you," Shae said getting teary eyed. Mrs. Watts patted her kindly on the back and left the room. Shae picked up the phone.

Charles's condition had upgraded to stable, and he'd been moved out of intensive care. She received the good news that the twins would be allowed visitors the next day. She relayed that to Toby.

"I'm so glad they're all right. Mama- I just don't know what to say about her," he said.

Shae also contacted the detective who'd come to their place earlier that week. The news he relayed to her would have shocked anyone else; it only confirmed all the other horrible stories she knew of her mother.

Her grandmother had died from arsenic poison, too. Her mother had taken out a $100,000 insurance policy on them and wanted to collect the money. She'd admitted it all to the public defender.

They thanked Mrs. Watts for the use of the phone then went back to their apartment. The four walls felt as if they were closing in on them. The air was filled with gloom. The television stayed off because neither of them felt like watching it.

"Shae, do you remember Daddy?" Toby asked out of the blue.

"Yeah, a little. He was hardly around," she said.

"Probably 'cause Mama ran him off," he remarked.

"I know he drank a lot. When he did show up, he was usually wasted." Shae seemed deep in thought. "I do remember, it's vague, but when I was about three or four, he used to come home from work. We didn't live in the projects then," she added. She

143

wrinkled her face, trying to recall the details. "We lived in a tan colored house near where they built the interstate. Daddy would come home from work. Vivian and I would be waiting, watching for him out the window. When his car pulled up in the driveway, we'd rush outside and throw ourselves at him. He'd swoop us up in his arms and swing us around and around. We'd laugh and laugh. I remember being so happy." She sighed deeply. "Then, I guess he lost his job. He started drinking and everything changed."

"It didn't help thing with me on the way, huh?" He'd done the math; if she'd been about three or four that meant that he wasn't yet born. Mrs. Byrts had been carrying him.

"It wasn't your fault," she said. "He got another job, but it didn't pay as good as the one he'd been working on. After we lost the house, we moved here. I hated it. I guess the main reason Daddy didn't move in with us was because of Mama. The projects are made for single women with children. If he lived with us, she'd have to pay a higher rent because he worked."

"Well, he still didn't have to just dip," Toby said.

"I guess three were enough. When Mama got pregnant and had twins, he just couldn't take it. He split for good. Maybe it was for the best. They used to fight, and Mama would hit him with whatever she could get her hands on. You were too little to remember the fights."

"I wonder where he is now," Toby thought out loud.

"I don't know." Shae shrugged.

She'd given up on ever seeing their father again. He had written them off and for that she'd never forgive him. Maybe their lives would have turned out differently had he stuck around.

"Was Mama ever nice?" Toby asked.

"Yeah, she was up until we moved to the projects," she grimaced. "The projects will turn anybody's heart to stone."

"That don't give her no right to kill her family," Toby said. "She took out a $100,000 insurance policy on all of us. We would have been next." He shook his head. "I should have known something was up. As greedy as she is, she never ate none of them powdered donuts. Since when did she become all nice and generous, all of a sudden?"

"Somewhere along the way, her mind must have slipped." Shae really couldn't pinpoint the exact moment it happened. Once, Mrs. Byrts had actually been a good mother. The projects had changed that. She came home complaining about her job as a certified nursing assistant. She griped about having to wipe old folks' asses for very little pay. Lifting people made her back hurt. The Director of Nursing was a bitch that had it in for her. It had been one thing after the next. It hadn't been long before she'd begun drinking. That's when all hell broke loose. They learned from experience that their mother was a mean drunk and she drank nearly every day.

They reminisced for a while longer then Toby left the apartment. He said he couldn't stand being there because it brought back too many bad memories. Shae felt the same way, but she didn't have anywhere else to go. She could call Dana, but she'd rather die a slow death than to be with him, especially after what he'd done to her earlier. Instead, she sat on the couch, letting the deadly silence embrace the pain in her heart.

CHAPTER EIGHT

T wo days after their mother's arrest, a woman wearing a crisp, business suit with her hair pulled up in a French twist, knocked on the door. Shae answered, frowning at the stranger standing there. Every time some fancy dressed person came to their place, it always spelled trouble.

"My name is Mrs. Kendra King. I was sent by DCF," the woman informed.

"Who?" Shae asked.

"The Department of Children and Family Services. I'm here to discuss you and your brothers' living arrangements. Can I come inside, please?" Shae let her in with reservations. Taking off her Prada sunglasses, the woman surveyed the living room with a critical eye before she sat down. Noticing that she also carried a Prada handbag with a matching briefcase, Shae deemed her a snob. No one in the 'hood wore Prada.

"I have some issues that I have to go over with you," Mrs. King stated.

"Like what?" Shae crossed her arms and waited. She wouldn't feel comfortable sitting, so she remained standing.

"Like where the boys-" She glanced down at a file as she spoke. "-Charles and Chris will be living upon release from the hospital, as well as Toby," she added. Her keen eyes rested on Shae.

"I thought they would get to come home." Shae assumed that Toby, Charles and Chris would live with her, but apparently DCF didn't see it that way

"I'm afraid that won't be possible, er-" She looked back down at the file, "LaShae, is it?

"Shae."

"Shae. That's not a possibility. Since the boys were harmed while living here, it's considered an unsafe environment," she informed.

"But Mama is locked up. She can't hurt them again," Shae insisted.

"I understand," Mrs. King said, but in Shae's mind, she didn't *understand* anything.

"I can take care of the twins. I practically raised them from birth anyway. Mama was always gone, or drunk. When she was home, all she did was beat them and yell at them. I did everything for Chris and Charles. It was like they were my own kids instead of my brothers," she shared in a desperate attempt to get the woman to see her side of things.

"I'll take all that you've shared with me into consideration," the woman said once they'd finished talking.

She'd read the hospital record on the twins as well as the statements given to the police department by Shae and Toby. She didn't doubt that the mother had been a vicious woman and an uncaring mother. And who could tell how the daughter would turn out? Regardless, it wasn't feasible in her mind that an eighteen-year-old could raise three children.

"You must understand that we want what's best for the children. Do you sincerely feel that living in the projects is the ideal life for them? There's drug dealing, shootings, prostitution, as well as other types of danger." She gathered her files together, shoved them into the briefcase, and snapped it shut. "I sincerely doubt that the state will give their approval for you to be their legal guardian," she informed as she stood.

"Why not?" Shae asked.

"Well, first of all, do you have a job?" the woman questioned.

"No."

"Did you even finish high school?" she inquired with a frown.

"No but-"

"How will you support the children?" she went on.

"I don't know. I'll get a job and-"

"What type of skills do you have?" the woman pressed.

"Well- I- I can be a waitress or something," Shae said in desperation. Mrs. King gave her a pitying look. Shae dropped her head in shame.

"Your brother, Toby, is he here? I have instructions to remove him from the home within forty-eight hours."

"I don't know where he is," Shae lied.

The woman's sharp eyes didn't blink even though she knew it was a lie. She'd dealt with this type of situation often and had learned to read people well.

"I'll be back once the agency reviews your case file. As I mentioned, we will take everything into consideration. We have to look out for the best interest of the children." She put her shades back on and tucked the briefcase underneath her arm, an indication that the meeting had ended.

Shae walked her to the door, showing her out.

"Have a nice day." She walked off, and Shae could hear the sound of her high heels clicking down the sidewalk. Apparently she had more than one family to visit in the projects since her car remained parked out front. No doubt, some other family would be torn apart before the day ended.

"Fucked up, huh?" Shae turned to find Toby standing on the stairway. "I heard everything," he told her. "I ain't going. If DCF want to take me somewhere, they gonna have to catch me. I know what happens in foster homes. You got a lot of sick, twisted motherfuckers acting like they are about children. They just want to have an easy way to abused and molest kids. They ain't gonna fuck my life up. Shit, it's already fucked up enough." He headed for the kitchen. "None of us will ever see each other again, either."

"They don't even care about breaking apart a family. We're all we got. I don't want us broken apart, spread all over the place," Shae said in distress.

"Like I said," Toby repeated "They'll have to catch me. And if they do, I'll run away again. That's real." He went back upstairs carrying a large bowl of Fruit Loops.

Shae sat down. She bit the corner of her lip as she thought. What would happen once DCF separated them? Would she forget that her brothers even existed? She didn't think she could ever forget all that had happened to them. Could she be like her sister Vivian, and never look back? It couldn't be that easy. Too much had taken place, and it all would remain etched in her memory forever. Her brothers were an extension of her. Losing them would be like losing a part of self. Tears of helplessness slid down her cheeks. She could do absolutely nothing about their situation.

Shae received the news that the twins wouldn't be allowed to live with her. It came delivered in a large, yellow envelope with the word CONFIDENTIAL stamped on it in bold, red letters. She'd already known, in a sense, but wasn't ready to accept it. It didn't help her case when she missed the court date. She couldn't make it to the hearing because Dana gave her a black eye. Showing up asking for custody of her brothers in that condition would have been a huge mistake.

She opened the envelope and read the letter. The story was the same: she was too unstable to care for them. Of course, the letter reiterated the fact that they were looking out for the "best interest of the children." She'd thought that telling them she'd practically raised the boys by herself would make a difference, but it hadn't. The state took custody. Charles and Chris were placed in foster care upon release from the hospital.

Shae was devastated. She had lost everything she ever cared about. At least she still had Toby, and that consoled her a little. He would have been sentenced to the same fate, only he couldn't be found. When Mrs. King returned to remove him from the home, he and most of his clothing had disappeared. Shae had no idea where he was or how to get in contact with him.

As an adult, she could fend for herself. Just like that, she was on her own. She rented a room at a motel because if she remained at the apartment, Dana would find her. It wasn't quite the way she had wanted it, but at least she'd finally gotten out the projects.

She hadn't seen Dana since he'd blackened her eye, and was determined to avoid him at all cost. He'd put his hands on her for the last time. She wanted to leave the past behind her and considered him part of that past. She needed to make some sense of her life, at least what was left of it.

The money that she'd taken with her wouldn't sustain her forever. She'd left her life savings behind, not wanting to carry such a large amount around. She knew that people broke into hotel rooms all the time, and the maids couldn't be trusted not to rob you blind. She'd go back to the apartment and retrieve it as soon as the coast was clear. It would take a while before another family was allowed to move into the unit. The St. Petersburg Housing Authority had a waiting list as long as two years for the Section 8 program. Even though families desperately needed housing, the process to get into them was slow and grueling. Residents got placed at different times of the year. It would be at least six more months before that occurred. Shae wasn't worried because she'd have her money long before then.

The first week on her own, she only left the room to get something to eat. Even then, she didn't venture too far away from the hotel. Luckily for her, a KFC as well as a Chinese restaurant were located nearby. She kept a low profile because the last thing she wanted was to run into Dana. If he found her, she knew he'd attack her again for not contacting him in days. He'd probably even try to force her to live with him. She'd virtually be his slave. That would be a fate almost worse than death. She would not allow him to dictate her life. Her mother had already done that, and she refused to let anyone else do the same.

She left the car he'd given her parked in front of his place with a note under the windshield wiper.

151

Once he read it, he'd get the point. She wanted nothing more to do with him.

Another week passed. Shae felt she'd wasted enough time wallowing in self-pity. She had to pull herself together and find a job. Once she began working and found an apartment, she'd go before the courts and try to gain custody of her brothers. Being a responsible adult would be proof that she could care for them.

She dressed up in a nice business-casual skirt set and headed out. Even though she completed job applications most of the morning, she didn't have much luck. Not too many people wanted to hire a high school dropout with no work experience. The real world was harder to live in than she'd thought. She now had a clear understanding of what the DCF worker had been talking about. She had thought the snooty woman had been condescending, but now she knew better.

After searching and getting rejected over and over, depression settled over her. What was the problem? Sure, she'd dropped out of high school, but she wasn't dumb. Why couldn't anybody see that? Why wouldn't they give her a chance?

She went back to the hotel and lay across the bed, feeling sorry for herself. If she didn't find something soon, she'd be forced to result to desperate measures. Dana had taken her to visit many nightclubs where women danced for money. She knew without a doubt that she could get hired as a stripper. She just didn't want to parade around half naked in front of men who slobbered out their mouths with lust. She shivered from the thought and pulled the sheet over her, closing her eyes in frustration.

TERESA D. PATTERSON

She'd almost fallen asleep when she heard a knock on the door. Automatically, she tensed. She feared that Dana had found her and didn't know what to do. He'd be steaming mad and she didn't want to face his wrath. Maybe, he'd just go away if she remained silent.

"Shae, are you in there?" She recognized Toby's voice. "Open up." She ran to the door and snatched it open.

"Toby, where have you been?" she exclaimed, happy to see him.

"Around," he answered and ambled into the room.

"Wait. How did you find me?" She hadn't let too many people know where she was staying.

"Aunt Bea told me, girl. Anyway, I got some good news."

"What?"

"Aunt Beatrice got custody of the twins. That's where they're staying." Shae threw her arms around his neck.

"That's great news. What about you?" she asked stepping back to look at him. Toby glanced down at his feet.

"She didn't want me," he finally answered. "It's not that she don't care- it's just that I'd be a bad influence on the other kids...selling drugs and all." He put his hands in his pockets. "It don't matter none. I can take care of myself."

"No, you can't. You're only fourteen. How can you make it out in the streets? You already got in trouble once. You're still selling drugs. There's danger all around you. If you go out there in the streets, you might get killed. I don't want that to happen."

153

"Shae, forget the speech," he interrupted rudely. "I'm here for another reason. I came to tell you what I know about that shooting." He took a deep breath. "Remember that day the twins had to go to the hospital and you and Dana stopped to pick me up at the store?" Shae nodded and he continued. "That's when I realized that Dana and Diamond Dog is the same person. Shae, Dana is the one who shot that junkie, Chancey. He's the big time drug dealer that I sell for."

"What. How you know that?"

"I started asking questions to some of the guys on the street. You see, we just get the stuff from somebody else. They found out it comes from Dana." Toby began to pace the room. "How can I turn him in?" he asked, near hysterics. "He'll kill me. The word out on the street is that he's looking for me now. I didn't do nothing. I ain't take no money or cheat him out of no drugs or nothing. I don't know what he want, but I ain't trying to find out." He stopped pacing abruptly. "I'm – I'm fucked. What if he wants to kill me, too? I don't want to die, man." His eyes seemed to beg his sister for help. He counted on her to keep him alive. Hadn't she protected him for most of his life?

"Toby, you and me are going down to the police station, now," she said. Even though that wouldn't be the type of revenge she'd wanted, it would satisfy her. She could turn Dana in now that she had something on him. He'd be behind bars where he couldn't rape or shoot anyone else.

"But, Shae-"

"No buts, Toby. Let's go. This is the only way to save you. If they lock him up, he can't get to you." He couldn't get to her either, but she kept that to herself.

"He got connections," Toby pointed out. "They'll come after me- and you."

"We'll get protection. It has to stop somewhere. Come on Toby. You can't take the fall for somebody else. You have to tell on him, and you have to do it today." Toby finally gave in and they went to the police station.

After Toby gave his statement, the police department immediately put out an APB on Dana Russell. It wasn't long before they caught up with him. News about his arrest spread like a forest fire throughout the projects. The newspapers carried the story, and the local stations broadcasted it on the six o'clock news. Shae and Toby watched the coverage, but they didn't dare breathe easily. It wasn't even halfway over. They knew that someone could find them at any given moment. They changed hotels several times to be on the safe side. Once things died down a bit, they began to feel less nervous.

***

Shae could sense Toby's restlessness. They'd been holed up inside the hotel room all week, and he was feeling claustrophobic. He complained that he needed some fresh air. Shae knew of his dilemma but could do nothing about it.

"I guess it's alright if you go to the store," she said after watching him fidget with the television, get up and pace the room, then go back to the TV. "We're out of milk. Just hurry back."

"Ain't nobody gonna bother me. You worry too much. I'll be right back," he said, putting on a brave face.

"Be careful," she warned.

"I will."

Shae heard gunshots five minutes after Toby left, and the blood in her veins froze. Her heart began pounding so rapidly in her chest that it hurt. When Toby burst through the door moments later, she let out the air she'd been holding in her lungs.

"They found me." Pure terror showed on his face.

"Did you get shot? Are you okay?" she asked frantically, rushing over to him to check.

"I'm gonna die. They found me," he kept saying over and over. He seemed to be in shock but other than that, fine. Shae smacked him in order to bring him to his senses.

"Get a grip, Toby," she yelled, shaking him firmly. He gained some amount of control but fear still consumed him. Shae ventured over to the window and peered through the Venetian blinds. "No one's out there. I think it was just a warning. We have to get moving as soon as possible. We had to leave St. Petersburg altogether." For some reason, she thought of Bradenton, across the Skyway Bridge. If she could, she'd leave the state. "You got any money?" she asked her brother who still stood in the middle of the floor as if paralyzed.

"N-no," he stuttered. "Not on me."

"Damn. Well, we have to go back to the apartment in the projects. All my money is hidden there and we need it," she said. "We have to go back."

That got a reaction from Toby. "I ain't going there, Shae. I'll be dead. That's Dana's territory." She understood and agreed. Even if Dana's people weren't there, there were snitches that would sell Toby out if they saw him. It didn't matter to them that they'd grown up with him. In the projects, there was no such thing as loyalty, especially if money got added to the equation.

"I'll go by myself. You just stay here." She stared at him and their eyes locked. "If I'm not back in an hour, call the police."

When she left, she heard the deadbolts on the other side of the door click into place. At least Toby would be safe. She wasn't so sure about herself. She hoped that she'd be able to sneak back into the apartment unnoticed since darkness had fallen. If anyone saw her, she'd go down too. Everybody was out for self.

Once she reached their former apartment, she turned the key in the lock and went inside. She didn't switch on a light for fear of drawing unwanted attention to the place. She felt her way up the stairs and to her old room. Once inside, she knelt in the corner and lifted the carpet. She felt for the money, but her hands groped emptiness. It wasn't there. Thinking that in her haste she'd missed it, she felt around again. Nothing.

"Is this what you want?" An evil voice shattered the quietness and sent pure terror through her. Light suddenly flooded the darkened room. Dana stood holding her life savings in his hands. "I got a feeling you'd be back for something. I'm glad I thought to stake this place out after I got released. You must be stupid if you thought I'd stay in jail. Money talks. Bullshit walks. Tonight is my lucky night." He waved the money in her face. "You got quite a bankroll here. A knot. What did you do to earn it?" he smirked.

Shae remained speechless. Her worst nightmare had become a reality. She was cornered, and Dana would never let her leave with the money.

"I think I have to teach you a lesson," he said. "Number one: you don't hide from me. Number two: you don't snitch on me to the cops. And number three: you don't use me. You did all three. Guess where that leaves you?" He aimed his index finger and thumb at her in the formation of a gun. "You think you can just write me a Dear John letter and end it? Nah. It don't work like that. It's not over until I say so." He'd been speaking in low tones. Suddenly he yelled, causing her to jump. "You could have had anything you wanted. Anything. Why you had to be such a greedy, stupid bitch?" He threw the wad of money in her face.

"I- I can explain," she stammered. "It's not what you think."

"Ain't no explaining nothing," he spat. "Come here. Come here, right now." She cowered in the corner. "Don't make me get mad," he barked. "Get over here. Now." She stood up on trembling legs and somehow wobbled over to him.

"I'm gonna fuck you one last time. I'm gonna fuck you like you ain't never been fucked before." Shae wanted to run, but she knew she wouldn't be able to get past him. She stared into his twisted face. How could she have ever thought he was handsome? He resembled a wild animal. "Get on ya knees bitch." He hit her, and she complied. "Turn around." He snatched her body around roughly and forced her into the doggy-style position. Not taking time to undress her, he hiked her skirt up and shoved her panties to the side. He surged into her from the back. Shae sucked in her breath from the shock of receiving the length of him. "You been trying to hide this pussy from me? Didn't I tell you that it belongs to me? Why you make me hurt you, huh? You must

158

like pain. Well, I'll give you just what you want." He grabbed her by the hair, yanking it. When she yelped, he slapped her on the ass cheeks and squeezed her nipples painfully. He bit her on the back of her shoulders and neck. He just seemed to go crazy. The more she cried out, the more animalistic he became. He shoved himself into her, howling like a werewolf as he reached climax.

Shae thought it would be over, but Dana wasn't quite finished. He pulled out of her and put his penis back in his pants. Shae straightened her underwear and stood up. She felt some of his sticky, hot semen oozing down her thigh. She tried to edge toward the door, only to be intercepted.

"Where you think you going? You gonna be sorry you ever crossed me. You might just end up like that junkie I fucked up." He pulled out a switchblade. "But shooting you would be too easy. You deserve to suffer for that shit you did." His voice changed, and she knew right then and there that he'd slipped over the brink of sanity. "You just like my mama, that no good fucking whore. She made my daddy kill her ass. He was right to kill that low down, cheating ass bitch." He nodded madly. "Yeah, he took care of her. He had to handle that. Just like I'm gonna take care of you." He looked at her and the wild look in his eyes turned into disgust. "You just a high yellow bitch with a lot of fucking hair. You know, ya looks 'bout all you got going for you. With no looks, you won't have too far to go." He snarled at her like a rabid dog getting ready to attack. "I wonder what you'd be like without ya looks. What if I just cut up that pretty, light skin? Huh? Put some marks in it? How 'bout that? Or ya hair?" He grabbed a handful of it and pulled, causing her scalp to burn. With a move

so swift that she didn't have time to blink, he
chopped off a great portion. She screamed when she
saw it hit the floor. "Shut up," he yelled as he
continued to yank and cut until nearly all of her hair
lay on the floor around her. She trembled in fear
when he held the blade up to her face. "You gonna
always remember me whenever you look in a mirror,"
he said as he brought the knife closer and pressed it
against her cheek.

"Please don't," she begged.

Suddenly, they heard feet trampling up the
stairs. Toby must have called the police. Shae
desperately hoped that they'd get to her in time. She
didn't want her face to be cut.

"God, please, help me," she silently prayed.

"Police! Freeze!" The cops burst into the room,
but Dana moved swiftly. She saw pure evil in his
eyes as he sliced her across her cheek with the sharp
blade. She screamed as she felt the sting of it cut
into her flesh. She continued to scream over and over
as he stabbed her.

Soon, the police were upon him. They drew their
revolvers and had their fingers on their triggers. In
the blink of an eye, they would blow him away. He
just chuckled insanely as he kneeled on the carpeted
floor.

"Arrest me motherfuckers cause she got what
she deserved," he said. To add insult to injury, he
spat across the room and the glob landed in her face.
"You just like my no good bitch ass mammy."

Shae drew her knees up and curled into a fetal
position. Dana's spittle mixed with her blood and
tears. At that moment, she really didn't care whether
she lived or died. She thought about Toby, Charles,
and Chris as she succumbed to darkness.

CHAPTER NINE

I t took weeks for Shae to regain consciousness. The strong smell of disinfectants invaded her nostrils, making her want to sneeze. Her throat felt dry and parched. She heard the beeps and clicks coming from different machines and knew she couldn't be at home.

Where am I? she wondered.

When she managed to peer through slits in her eyes, she saw nothing but whiteness. Doctors and nurses walked in and out of the room. The tubes that ran through her body prevented her from moving. When she tried, she felt excruciating pain.

She opened her mouth to voice her discomfort, but no words came out. A nurse wearing plastic gloves walked over to the bed, lifted her arm, and gave her a shot. She drifted off again. She flitted in and out of consciousness. During different intervals, she thought she saw Toby and the twins, but everything remained hazy. She no longer was certain of anything. She wasn't even sure if she was still alive.

Three more weeks passed. Finally, Shae opened her eyes. She looked around the room in confusion. It dawned on her that she was in the hospital. Why? Where was Toby? Was he safe? Could somebody come answer her questions?

The memories rushed at her. She heard the gunshots, and she remembered going back to the projects to get her money. Dana had been waiting and he tried to kill her.

She heard someone entered the room and turned to see who it was.

"Welcome back, young lady. You gave us quite a scare," a round-faced, white nurse chirped. She held a cotton alcohol swab in one hand.

"How long- have I- been here?" Shae managed to get past her parched lips. She wanted a drink of water.

"Do you really want to know?" The nurse rubbed the swab on Shae's upper arm. "You've been here quite a while- five weeks altogether." She brought forth a needle. "You're lucky to be alive."

"Ouch." The fat nurse had stuck her while she'd been distracted.

"Welcome back kid." The nurse smiled and placed a bandage over the small puncture. "I bet you'd like a drink." She held up a cup with water while Shae sipped from the straw. "All finished?" Shae nodded. The nurse returned the cup to the nightstand. "If you need anything, just push the call button," she advised then left.

Shae stared around the room again as she rubbed her sore arm. A vase of white lilies sat on a nearby table. They were beautiful, and she wondered who sent them. When a medical technician entered to check her vitals, Shae asked her to read the card.

"Pretty flowers," the young girl complimented. She smiled as she retrieved the card attached and opened it. "It says: These should have gone-" She stopped in mid-sentence.

"What?" Shae asked in alarm. She didn't like the horrified expression on the aide's face.

"-on your grave," she finished in a whisper. The card fell from her hands, fluttering to the floor as she hurried from the room.

After that incident, a security guard stood on post outside the door. Even though the flowers had been removed, their scent lingered. The sticky, sweet fragrance reminded Shae that it wasn't over. Dana wasn't finished with her yet.

The day came when all the tubes that invaded her body were removed. Shae sat up in bed and ran a hand through her hair. It hit her that it was cropped short, courtesy of Dana and his switchblade. She put her hands up to her face and gasped when she felt the scar on her cheek. She hit the call button, signaling for the nurse.

"Nurse," she screamed. "Nurse." She repeatedly pushed the button when no one came right away.

"What is it?" the bewildered nurse asked when she arrived to find Shae in such a frantic state.

"Bring me a mirror," Shae demanded.

"But-" The nurse hesitated. She didn't think the young girl should see the scar just yet. It had recently been stitched and looked worse than it actually was.

"Bring me a damn mirror. Now," she yelled. The nurse hurried from the room and returned moments later with a medium-sized hand mirror. Shae snatched it and held it up to her face.

"Oh God," she moaned. "No. No." A scream came from the bottom of her soul. She hurled the mirror as hard as she could across the room. It shattered into a thousand pieces when it hit the wall.

What she'd seen in the mirror remained permanently etched in her memory. She knew she'd never be the same. Gone was the beautiful girl she'd once been. All that was left was a scarred, grotesque monster. No one would ever want her now. Dana's evil words taunted her.

163

"You gonna always remember me whenever you look in a mirror."

She buried her face in the hospital pillow and cried hysterically. She had to be given a shot to sedate her.

Shae settled into a deep depression. She refused to eat and remained unresponsive for weeks. She wanted to die, but they wouldn't even allow her to do that in peace. Instead, they assigned her to some new physician named Dr. David Michaels. He made her sick. She just wanted him to go away and stop bugging her, but he wouldn't.

Dr. Michaels knew that he got on his patient's last nerves. He refused to leave her alone and he forced her to talk, even if it was just to swear. If it meant she'd get better, she could curse at him from sun up until sun down.

LaShae Byrts was one patient that he wouldn't lose. He'd recognized her potential and worked with determination to make her regain her will to live. If she wanted to die, he was afraid she wouldn't be doing it on his watch.

His heart went out to the young woman. He'd examined the lengthy patient chart and knew everything about her. It was enough to make anyone want to curl into the fetal position and die. But, Dr. Michaels had decided that would not be an option for LaShae Byrts. He'd give her a little more time to pull it together. If he saw that she wasn't attempting to recover, he'd step in and intervene.

"Good morning. Rise and shine, Sunshine."
When Shae heard the familiar voice of Dr. Michaels, she groaned. She wanted to pull the sheet over her face. He approached the bed and gazed down at her. "Okay, young lady. I think you've been allowed to wallow in self-pity long enough. It's time you got back to doing some serious living." The middle-aged, black doctor gave Shae a stern look. "You're being discharged tomorrow." He pushed the button on the automatic bed and it raised her up to a sitting position.

"What?" Shae glared at him in annoyance. He'd been coming to check on her every day. He fussed at her about eating to build up her strength. No matter how much she resisted, saying that she wasn't hungry or the hospital food tasted disgusting, he kept insisting that she needed nourishment. So, she ate just to shut him up.

He'd even had the nerve to tell her that she looked a mess. He suggested that she fix herself up a bit. At first she'd been angry. She was in a hospital, not in a runway model competition. After the anger subsided, she managed to put on something other than a hospital gown.

Even when she didn't want to talk, he sat by her bed and asked question after question. She'd cursed him out profusely, but it hadn't made him leave. He just kept coming back. Every day, she'd see his annoying face and groan. Now, here he stood telling her she had to leave.

"You heard me. I said, you're being sent home tomorrow," he repeated.

"But I'm not ready to go yet," she protested.

"LaShae Byrts, you're fine. Your wounds are practically healed. You're perfectly capable of taking care of yourself. As a matter of fact, you've been able to leave here weeks ago. It's time you faced reality and stopped feeling sorry for yourself."

"Who the hell are you to tell me what I'm able to do?" Shae yelled. "I can't go out there."

"You can," he stated firmly.

"You don't understand. You ain't the one who have to walk around looking like a-" She wanted to say "freak" but couldn't bring herself to utter the harsh word. That's exactly what she'd seen when she looked in the mirror.

"Like a person that's been cut?" he finished for her. "Dear, that mark on your face is barely noticeable. In time, it will disappear completely. If you want, I can recommend one of the best plastic surgeons in the state. But, that's the least of your worries." He grasped her chin in a firm grip and forced her to look at him. "Don't be a coward. You're afraid to go out there because you think you'll fail. You've known nothing but disappointment all your life. So, disappointment is what you expect." Shae wanted to flinch from his hurtful words, but she held his gaze, unblinking. "I know I've been rather hard on you. But, I won't let you give up on yourself. I've seen your brothers come here every day to visit you. I've seen your aunt, too. They wouldn't come if they didn't love you. Show them that you love them, too. They are counting on you. Don't just give up. You are not a weak person. You've endured too much to just succumb to obstacles now. Be the strong, beautiful, black woman that you are. Get out of this bed and embrace life. You've been given a second chance, you know?" He let go of her chin, but she still didn't look away. "Think about what I've said, young lady." He walked off, turned to look at her one last time, then left.

Shae did nothing but think all day long. At five that evening she'd made up her mind. She decided not to wait until the following day. She wanted to leave as soon as possible. The doctor's words had a profound effect on her. She and her brothers didn't have the best life, but she could strive to make it better. In order to do that, she had to get busy living.

She picked up the phone and called Toby. Her trip home required clothes and she needed him to bring them. Once she got out of the hospital bed, she'd be leaving for good. Aunt Beatrice had welcomed her with opened arms. Even though the law considered Shae an adult, Aunt Bea wasn't trying to hear of her struggling or living in a hotel.

"You come stay with me until you get on ya feet, you hear?" she'd insisted when she'd last visited. Shae was finally ready to accept her aunt's offer.

First, she needed to thank Dr. Michaels for pointing her in the right direction and for all of his encouragement. Never had anyone cared about her that much.

It surprised Dr. Michaels when he looked up from his desk and saw Miss Byrts enter his office. She wore a very feminine dress and even had on heels. She looked beautiful with her short, curly hair and high cheekbones.

"Hi," she said, suddenly at a loss for words because she'd picked up on the appreciation in his eyes. "I just wanted to say thank you. You- you were right."

"Just doing my job," he stated modestly. "Besides, I couldn't let such a lovely lady just waste away."

"You're only saying that because you're my doctor." She stared at her feet. "I'll never be pretty again."

"Stop it," he chided. "Come here." He ushered her toward a mirror.

"No," she said, shaking her head. "I can't look." She remembered the last time she'd seen her reflection. She didn't want to experience that horror again.

"Come on." He gave her a gentle push forward. She covered her eyes with her hands, not brave enough to look. "Look at yourself. I'm telling you, the scar is almost gone. When you saw yourself the first time, it wasn't healed. The cut was still fresh and had just been stitched up. It's healed now. I removed the stitches, and you look fine. Go ahead, take a look." He pulled her hands away from her eyes. "See?" She held her breath and looked.

"Oh?" She stared in surprise. It wasn't at all what she expected. Once again, Dr. Michaels was right. The scar was no bigger than half an inch, resembling a scratch.

"Well?" he asked. "What do you have to say? I'm the one who stitched you up. Some pretty good handiwork, huh?"

"It's- it's not as bad as I thought," she finally said. "Thank you." Grateful tears fell from her eyes. She wasn't ugly and scarred for life, as she'd assumed. Once she started, she couldn't seem to stop the flow. "I'm s-sorry," she sobbed, covering her face in embarrassment. "I can't stop cry-"

"It's alright," he soothed. "Just let it all out. It's okay." He held her in his arms, patting her on the back. "Everything will be just fine. You're over the hump."

When she stopped crying, Dr. Michaels went over to his desk and grabbed a box of Kleenex. "Here," he offered.

"Thank you." She took a tissue and dabbed at her eyes. Somewhat composed, she turned to him. "I didn't mean to break down like that."

"It's okay." He smiled. "There's no need to apologize."

"It's just that everything came back to me all at once," she explained.

"I understand," he said quietly and somehow she felt that he really did. On an impulse, she threw her arms around his neck and gave him a hug.

"Thank you for everything, Dr. Michaels. I couldn't leave without telling you that." She smiled. It was the first real smile he'd seen from her, and it brightened the whole room. "Bye."

"Good-bye, Miss Byrts. Take care of yourself and those brothers of yours."

He watched her walk away, thinking: *If only I were twenty years younger.* He shook his head and picked up his cup of coffee. He felt confident that she'd do just fine. After all, she was a fighter and a survivor.

Shae had been living with her aunt for a week when she decided it was time to move. With the twins, as well as her four cousins, Aunt Beatrice's house was filled to capacity. They had no privacy and not a moment of silence. Shae felt that at eighteen, she needed to depend on herself. Her aunt had

169

already done so much, taking in Chris and Charles so that the family wouldn't be separated. She had to make it on her own. She wanted to prove that she could take care of her brothers so she could gain custody of them. She wouldn't be happy until they were all under the same roof again, and that included Toby.

They finished eating the big breakfast that Aunt Beatrice cooked. Shae cleared the dishes off the table. "Charles and Chris are you ready to go to the bus stop?" she asked. Both boys nodded enthusiastically, and Shae smiled. They'd eaten pancakes with log cabin syrup and had syrupy mustaches. "Well, let me get a wash cloth to clean ya sticky faces."

After Shae cleaned their hands and faces, they headed off. The bus stop was only a block away. Charles skipped along, and Chris stopped to pick up rocks. It made her happy to see them behave like six year old boys. She knew they hadn't had a good life up until that point, but now everything had changed. She couldn't imagine the extent of emotional damage that their mother's abuse had caused. She hoped that in time, they would be able to forget.

She watched as Chris and Charles got safely on the school bus. They waved at her until the bus turned the corner, and she could no longer see them. She went back to Aunt Bea's and settled down at the kitchen table with the classified ads in front of her. She looked under the "apartments for rent" section and saw one located in a decent area of the neighborhood.

"Shae, I'm off to work," her aunt called, heading for the front door.

"Aunt Bea?" Her aunt stopped, came back and peered into the kitchen.

"Yes child?"

"Can I borrow your car? I see an apartment for rent that I want to check out."

Her aunt gave her a tired but sweet smile. She knew that her niece was struggling to deal with so much at one time. She was glad to help with whatever she could. Someone so young shouldn't have to go through such hard times. To handle so many problems took the patience of Job. She prayed that Shae would be able to get through the trials and tribulations. She knew people who were supposedly deeply rooted in Christ who gave up when put through less. She'd always believed: whatever didn't kill you, made you stronger. Shae would come out of this on top and become a better person than before. God had *His* reasons.

"Come on and drop me off," she said, holding out the keys to her niece.

Shae loved Aunt Beatrice. She really was a kind woman, nothing at all like her sister, Bertha. The fact that they were identical twins was almost unimaginable.

She grabbed the classified section, got up from the table, and took the keys that her aunt extended.

As they drove toward their destination, Aunt Beatrice's mind drifted. She felt a deep sadness that her twin sister had turned out to be such a bad seed. She knew Bertha began drinking heavily and that she was emotionally disturbed. She just hadn't known how deeply disturbed she was. Something had changed inside her after Jimmy left.

She couldn't help but wonder if there was something she could have done to prevent anything that had happened. If only she had known. But, she'd chosen not to know.

Beatrice had stopped visiting Bertha many years before. She hadn't agreed with the way she disciplined her children, and one day she'd voiced her disapproval. She'd never forget that day. It happened when she found out Shae's arm had been broken. She confronted Bertha after seeing her niece's cast.

"What that baby do to make you hurt her like that?" Beatrice demanded to know.

"She called the ambulance and now everybody knows my business. You know I don't like airin' our dirty laundry. She best be keepin' her mouth closed 'bout things that happen around here."

"What was she supposed to do, just let her sister bleed to death, Bert? What you did to both of them children is just plain wrong. How can you look at ya self in the mirror?"

"I done told you to mind ya own damn business 'bout how I raise my children." Bertha's voiced escalated. The two sisters eyed each other, neither ready to back down from a confrontation.

"Don't you raise ya voice at me." Beatrice who was usually calm and mild mannered got fed up. It seemed there was no way to reason with her sister. Now she was hot. "Somebody need to take 'em away from you. You don't deserve to have children that you gone beat and abuse every day. You use them children as ya punching bag. It ain't their fault Jimmy B left you. Stop treating 'em like it is."

"Now, Bea, you 'bout to make me tell you something I'll regret. You buttin' in where it don't concern you. Jimmy B ain't got nothing to do with this conversation."

"Jimmy B got everything to do with it. You been like this ever since he left you. You started drinking like a camel, hanging in juke joints and whipping on them kids. You wasn't like that before and you *know* I know."

"Bea, what I do is my own damn business. Don't make me have to tell you again. If you don't like the way I do things, then you don't have to come 'round here," Bertha yelled at the top of her lungs.

"That's just fine with me," Beatrice yelled back, glaring at her twin. She got up and placed her hands on her hips. Beatrice wasn't a small woman by far. Even though she wasn't as heavy as her sister, she carried a few extra pounds. Her voice had an edge to it when she spoke. "If I hear 'bout you hurting them kids again, I might catch a charge for stomping a knot on ya ass," she warned. "Mama and Papa didn't raise you to be like this. You was raised in the church, and you know better. The devil done got in you. You need Jesus."

Bertha's face turned red and she jumped up from the kitchen table, overturning the chair in the process. She kicked it to the side and pointed toward the door.

"You, Jesus, and every damn body else better get the fuck out my house."

"Calm down, Bertha. Let's talk about this."

"Calm down my ass." She bent to pick up the overturned chair and raised it in the air. "I said get the fuck out of here and I mean it," she yelled.

"Put that chair down. I'm leaving. You have disrespected me for the last time," Beatrice said, giving her sister a pitying look.

PROJECT QUEEN

"Don't let the doorknob hit you where the good Lord split you," Bertha insulted, slamming the door behind her.

Bertha could be so unreasonable, stubborn and mean-spirited. Beatrice left in anger, and she hadn't returned since.

No, Beatrice hadn't been able to stand her sister for quite a few years now. She'd thought about turning her over to Protective Services, but in the black community that would have been frowned upon. You just don't do that to your own blood. Instead, she'd done whatever she could to help from a distance. Now, she just wished she'd done more. Her lack of involvement had probably attributed to Ma Violet's death. For that, she'd always feel regret. It would have to be faced and dealt with on Judgment Day.

Raising four children wasn't an easy task. Her husband died in a freak accident five years before. He'd been killed on the job when a crane fell on him. The money that she'd received from his life insurance policy sustained them to a certain extent.

Beatrice wasn't one to sit around and wait for a government check. As a matter of fact, she worked at Social Services and had for fifteen years. The little money she got from her job and her husband's check each month kept their heads above water. The monthly bills seemed overwhelming, and she was determined to put her oldest daughter through college.

Brenda had recently graduated high school and planned to attend FAMU the following semester. Even though she'd received an academic scholarship,

TERESA D. PATTERSON

there still was tuition and books as well as personal
expenses that required money. Plus, she needed a
car to get around. Beatrice was looking into buying
her a used one. Along with a car came insurance
payments. Always some other expense that had her
finances stretched to the limit.

Taking in two more children put a strain on her
budget. But Chris and Charles deserved a good life.
Since she'd failed them before, she wouldn't make
the same mistake twice. No way would she let them
live in a foster home. She felt she owed them that.
After all, they were her flesh and blood and she loved
them.

Toby was a different story. She loved her
nephew, but as long as he traveled on the wrong
path, he had to travel it alone. When he stopped
dealing drugs, her doors would be opened to him as
well.

Shae pulled up in front of the building where
Beatrice worked.

"Don't worry about picking me up, baby," Aunt
Bea told her. "I'll catch a ride with Ida or SueElla."

"Are you sure, Aunt Bea?"

"Yeah, baby. You just take ya time. If that one
apartment don't work out, don't give up. If it's God's
will, it's already done."

"Thank you, Aunt Bea."

Shae pulled off, thinking that her aunt was an
angel. Aunt Bea had always been the one to take up
for them back in the day. She had often wished that
Aunt Bea had been their mother instead. Shae
wasn't mad at her aunt for not coming around
because she knew her mama had run her off. She'd
been hiding behind the couch, listening to their

conversation the last time Aunt Bea stopped by. Shae had cried herself to sleep thinking that it was her fault they wouldn't see Aunt Bea anymore.

Fate had a way of turning things around. Now, they all lived with Aunt Beatrice, except for Toby. He'd stopped by Aunt Bea's house wearing a bunch of expensive jewelry and a removable gold grill. Aunt Bea's disappointment was evident by her deep frown. Shae had tried once again to talk him out of selling drugs, but had been unsuccessful. He shrugged her off saying he had to do what he had to do.

Aunt Bea remained adamant in her decision about Toby not living in the home. If Toby wanted to deal drugs, he had to sleep somewhere else. She didn't condone it and wouldn't have it in her home. Shae couldn't fault her for that decision.

She saw Toby from time to time when he stopped by. The last time she'd seen him, he looked so thin and tired. She'd asked him where he'd been staying.

"I'm at Raymond's place for now," he told her. Even though she was happy that he wasn't living on the streets, the location didn't impress her. Raymond's place was a known drug trap. Toby couldn't remain there for too long. The cops would probably raid it sooner or later. She had to find a place so that she could help her brother and possibly save his life.

***

Toby was at Raymond's house nodding off in a broken down La-Z-Boy chair. Everybody and their mama lived at Raymond's house, it seemed. People came and went like it was the 24-hour Wal-Mart. Toby stayed up most nights because the crack heads never slept. Besides, there wasn't anywhere to sleep at Raymond's. He'd be damned if he'd squeeze in the bed with four other grown ass Negroes. The couch, if you could call it that, was out of the question. It had all types of stains, and it reeked of urine and who knows what else. Plus, the house was infested with roaches. One night he'd been nodding in the chair and one of them mugs had crawled in his ear. He had to find somewhere else to crash before he fell out from exhaustion.

Aunt Bea's house was always neat and clean. She had plenty of food, and it was peaceful and quiet. He found himself going there almost every day. He made sure that he didn't have any drugs on him when he was there. He couldn't disappoint Aunt Bea anymore than he already had. He knew she only wanted the best for him. That's why she kept on him about the drug dealing. He wanted to stop, but he didn't want to be considered a punk.

He gazed around Raymond's place, frowning. Well, maybe he'd be a punk. He needed to take a shower, eat, and get some real sleep. If he could go to Aunt Bea's and do that, he wasn't worried about what the next common thug thought. All he cared about was getting off the streets. He was so tired of selling drugs anyway. It didn't take a genius to slang crack cocaine. Some of the so-called ballers that he hung with had dropped out of high school, too. Now, selling drugs was all they had to fall back on. Some of the ones who still had a heart advised him to get back in school. They told him that he didn't want to be selling drugs for the rest of his life.

"Man, you still young. You ain't got no felonies. Go back to school. This ain't no kinda life fuh you, dawg," a guy named Black advised.

177

"Black tellin' you the truth," Big Rob stated. "It's hard out here. You don't hafta do this shit tho' 'cause you still got a future. Me and most of these cats out here slangin', this all we got to fall back on. But you can be betta than this. You *are* betta than this. Get it together, partner, this ain't the life fuh you."

At the time, he hadn't been trying to hear what Black and Big Rob had been saying. But now he knew they were right. He felt so frustrated about his situation. But, he had a way out. Aunt Bea would help if he would just let her. Could he just walk away from the easy money?

A roach crawled across his arm, and he flicked it off in disgust. His mind was made up. Toby got up from the chair and headed for the door.

"Where you off to, man?" someone asked. Toby wasn't sure who the person was. So many different people crashed at Raymond's place.

"I'm out," he said.

"You got somethin', dawg?" The man stared at him with a desperate look in his eyes. Toby shook his head. He should have known it was a bass head. If Raymond wasn't careful, he was going to end up getting jacked. Trusting a crack head in your house was like trusting a hungry dog with a T-bone steak.

"Nah. You have to get up with Ray or somebody else."

"You got some weed? Anything?" he said through cracked, parched lips.

"Nah."

"A cigarette? Don't leave me hangin'. I need somethin' bad."

"Didn't I just tell ya fuck ass I ain't got nothing on me?" Toby said in frustration. "You need to leave that shit alone and straighten up ya life anyway."

178

"Fuck you." The junkie curled up on the couch. "All you had to do was say no, nigga." Toby couldn't believe how smoking crack could make a person look so rough. The man was shaking like he was freezing, and it had to be at least eighty degrees outside. If Toby's mind hadn't been made up before about leaving it all alone, it was made up now. He couldn't stand to see anybody looking so pitiful. The man's hair was matted. His clothes were filthy with dirt. He wore shoes that were caked with slime, and Toby could see his toes peering out. He smelled horrible, too. From the looks of it, he couldn't be more than a hundred pounds. If he kept smoking crack, he would eventually disappear.

"Don't die like this, man." Toby said, touching the guy on his thin shoulder. "Don't you have family-anybody, you can ask for help?"

"No." The man's tearful eyes met his. "Do you?" he asked through his cracked lips.

"Yeah, man. I do. And I want to thank you for helping me realize it." He released the man and walked out of Raymond's house for good.

* * *

Shae drove to the address she'd circled in the classifieds. A middle-aged gentleman was outside in the front yard painting the picket fence. He gazed up from what he was doing when he heard her car.

"Excuse me. Are you the owner?" Shae asked as she walked up.

"Yes. Did you come to look at the apartment?" He stopped painting and gazed up at her.

"Well, I-"

"Come on. I'll show it to you." He placed the paintbrush in a bucket and straightened up. "Follow me." His quick strides made Shae have to almost run to keep up. "It's an upstairs apartment. Two bedrooms, but I'm offering it at a reasonable price," he added. He fumbled with his key ring until he found the right one.

"How much are you renting it for?" Shae asked.

"Four hundred and fifty dollars per month." He opened the door. "See it for yourself and tell me if that's not reasonable."

Shae looked around. The large living room had hardwood floors that shined. It smelled as though the walls had been recently painted. The kitchen looked cozy with a modern stove, refrigerator and other appliances. She checked out the bathroom and was satisfied that it had been renovated as well. The two bedrooms also met her approval.

"I'll take it," she told him.

"But I haven't installed the washer and dryer yet."

"I'll take it anyway," she said excitedly and laughed. "I love it already. I'll take it." The old man looked at her like she'd lost her mind, but he seemed pleased.

"All I'm asking for is a security deposit up front," he told her. "You can pay the first month's rent at your convenience."

"It's no problem. I can pay it all now." She got the money from her purse, glad to be getting rid of it. One of the cops on the scene had gathered the money and put it in her purse on the night Dana almost killed her.

"Well, the place is yours." The old man smiled. "It doesn't matter to me what you do or who you have over, as long as you pay your rent on time. I'm a pretty fair judge of character and you seem to be a very respectable young lady. By the way, my name is

Stanley O'Conner. Just let me know if you need help moving in. I have three, healthy sons. One of them is about your age. Dale, he's eighteen. My other son, David, is twenty-one, and my oldest, Daniel, is twenty-three. They are all into that body-building thing," he relayed. "Here's your set of keys. I'll go get your lease agreement then I'll leave you alone." Shae smiled as he closed the door. She couldn't wait to tell Toby. He'd be so glad to have a permanent place to live.

Grateful that she had the use of her aunt's car, Shae drove to a discount furniture store and spent some more of the money buying furniture for the apartment. The store promised to deliver everything before the close of business.

Thankfully, she didn't have to go search for her brother. When she returned to Aunt Bea's house, she found him sitting at the kitchen table eating.

"Toby, I got good news," she said excitedly. He looked up from a bowl of cereal.

"What's that?"

"I found us an apartment. I bought furniture and everything."

"Us? You mean, I get to stay there?" he asked.

"Of course. Where else you gonna stay?"

"I don't know. It's just that- it's like a dream. I've been from friend to friend. I was running out of places to spend the night. I'm so glad I don't have go back to Raymond's." He looked relieved and happy. "When do we move in?" he asked.

"Real soon. I have to be there when the furniture truck shows up."

"All right." All the strain he'd been under for the past few months made him look older than fourteen. Shae noticed that he had grown a mustache and the beginnings of a beard. What had happened to the little boy she'd known as her brother? He'd grown up without her even noticing it.

"We'll leave after I talk to Charles and Chris," she told him.

"Okay." He got up to place the empty bowl in the sink.

Shae explained to the twins why she couldn't take them with her. Even though she wanted them to live in the same household, at that time, it wasn't possible. She promised to come by to see them every day.

She wasn't concerned about Charles and Chris's welfare, because Aunt Bea was a great caregiver. There certainly was a lot of love in that house, and the boys had blossomed since moving in. They constantly laughed aloud which was music to Shae's ears. She realized that back in the projects Charles and Chris hadn't been allowed to be little boys. They'd always been afraid that their mother would beat them if they made too much noise. Their innocence had been stifled. Now, they could just be kids without having to worry about anything. Their childhood wouldn't be snatched away like hers had been.

She felt a sense of pride of having her own apartment. She decorated it nicely with a leather sofa and loveseat. A moderate sized coffee table set in the middle of a zebra print rug. Different colored, scented candles rested in candleholders on two end tables. She hung cheerful curtains and added decorative pillows to the sofa. She even put up family photos that reminded them of happier times.

A few weeks after they moved into their own place Toby surprised Shae with an announcement. She'd noticed that he hadn't been hanging out late every night. He'd gotten rid of the gold-plated grill and didn't wear his pants hanging off his butt anymore. He no longer associated with his old friends. She saw that as a good sign.

"Do you think it's too late for me?" he asked. He leaned against the door jam and stared at her.

"Too late for what?" She stopped brushing her hair, which had grown long enough for her to pull back into a ponytail.

"To go back to school." She turned from the mirror to stare at him in surprise. "I think I want to go back. I don't want to sell drugs the rest of my life. I ain't no dummy. I know I can finish school."

"I'm glad you made up ya own mind. I wasn't going to run my mouth, but I do think it's a good idea. We'll go to the school and check into getting you reenrolled."

"Good. You know what? I might even go to college. I'm thinking 'bout becoming a doctor, like Dr. Michaels." His voice held conviction.

"I think you'll be a fine doctor. One of the best," she told him, and meant it.

The following day they went to Tyrone Middle School and completed the necessary paperwork to get Toby back in school. Since it was a different zone, Toby wouldn't be returning to his old school, which was a good thing. It would be better for him to get a fresh, new start. He didn't need to mix with his old friends and settle back into bad patterns.

It would be tough to fit in at a new school, but Toby was determined. Shae finished signing the papers and got up to leave.

"I'll see you when you get home. Okay?" she told him. He nodded and she left him sitting in the office until classes started. He looked nervous, but when she caught his eye through the window, he smiled. She smiled back and waved at him.

She caught PSTA, the city's bus transportation to downtown St. Petersburg. She wanted to put the rest of the money she had in a bank account. She got off the bus on Central Avenue and went inside Union First Bank. There seemed to be a shortage of tellers, so she asked if they needed help.

"As a matter of fact, we do," the young woman behind the glass partition, told her. Shae asked for an application and sat down to complete it. When she handed it back to the young lady, she was asked to wait.

"I'll see if you can be interviewed now." The woman smiled and Shae smiled back. She picked up the phone and spoke briefly. "You can go through that door and turn left," she informed. "Mrs. Watson will interview you today."

"Thank you."

"You're welcomed and good luck!"

Shae went through the door that had been pointed out. Twenty minutes later, she walked out with a job. Now she would need new clothes. Being in no hurry to go back home, she decided to do some shopping. She'd get a chance to write her first check!

She felt happy as she crossed the street to go into a clothing store. She wasn't paying attention to where she was walking and bumped into someone.

"Sorry," she said quickly and looked up into the face of the woman she'd collided with. The woman stared back at her almost fearfully. Shae recognized that face. Before she could say anything, the lady hurried off.

"Vivian!" Shae called and ran to catch up with her. She pulled on her sleeve and the woman turned around. Her face was void of all emotion. "Vivian?" Shae asked, tentatively. "Is it you?"

"I'm sorry, but you have the wrong person." She tried to pull away.

Shae knew that it was Vivian. It was her sister that she hadn't seen for more than six years. She'd know her own sister anywhere. She couldn't be mistaken, so she tried again.

"Vivian, it's me- your sister Shae. Remember?" The lady stared at her for a moment.

"I'm sorry," she repeated. "I don't know anyone by that name." She finally disengaged herself from Shae's grip. "If you'll excuse me, I have to be going now."

"Vivian, wait!" The lady stepped into the crowd and Shae lost sight of her. Somehow, she knew that it had been her sister. Why had Vivian pretended not to know her? Could she really have forgotten her own sister?

Shae walked on. Maybe it hadn't been Vivian after all. The woman didn't have a scar where Vivian would have one from being shoved into the mirror. But the eyes had been the same as well as the rest of her features.

"I know what my sister looks like," Shae said aloud. She was convinced that she'd seen Vivian and her gut feeling told her that it was true.

Shae had been to quite a few stores. For some unknown reason she decided to stop at the shop on the corner. Struggling with all of her packages, she pushed open the door and entered. Right away she spotted the woman behind the counter. Vivian.

Shae felt determined to get to the bottom of why her sister had acted like she didn't know her. No matter how she had tried to convince herself that it hadn't been Vivian, something within her told her that it was. She was going to find out for sure. She approached the counter.

"May I help-" The woman's smile froze when she saw Shae, but she quickly composed herself. "May I help you?" she finished.

"I know you're my sister," Shae told her. "Why are you acting like you don't know me, Vivian?"

"That is not my name," the woman stated in a harsh tone. "My name is Vanessa. I don't know anyone named Vivian. I told you that earlier. Why don't you stop harassing me?" She turned away to wait on a customer. When she finished and the customer left the store, Shae tried again.

"Vivian- I mean, Vanessa. I don't know why you're acting like this, but I want to tell you that Mama's in jail." She watched the woman's face. "She tried to poison the twins. And she killed Ma Violet." She could see some reaction in the lady's eyes. The woman looked away but Shae continued. "I was in the hospital for a while. I got involved with a drug dealer and he tried to kill me." She touched her hair self-consciously. "That's why my hair is shorter. He-he cut it off and he cut my face," she added. The lady glanced at the tiny scar that was still visible then looked away again. "Toby had got into some trouble, quit school, and started selling drugs. But he straightened out." She paused. "I got us a small apartment, and I even got a job today at the bank." She waited for the woman to speak, but when she

186

didn't, Shae picked up her bags and began to back away. "I just thought I'd let you know. I'm glad I got a chance to see you again." Her voice caught in her throat. "If you're not Vivian, then I'm sorry I bothered you." She turned to leave.

"Wait," the lady called when Shae reached the door. Shae stopped and turned around to face her. "I am- Vivian," she said softly. She looked at her younger sister with compassion. "Let's go somewhere to talk. Wait one second." She spoke briefly with another woman who was busy attaching price tags to clothes. The lady nodded and Vivian went to join Shae. "There's a park not too far away," Vivian told her. "Let's go there."

As they walked, Shae told her about how she'd gotten involved with Dana, how he'd raped her, and then how he'd tried to kill her.

"Oh, how awful for you," her sister sympathized.

"I was stupid," Shae said. "Looking for an easy way out of the projects almost cost me my life and Toby's."

"How could you have known?" Vivian asked.

"I was just so desperate! Mama kept getting worse and worse. Sometimes, I wanted to hurt her!"

"It's normal, under the circumstances, to have those types of feelings," Vivian told her.

"I saw Dana as my way out. I should have concentrated on going back to school or on getting a job. I wish I could change things."

"Thankfully, that's all in the past now," Vivian told her in a gentle tone. "It's up to you to let go of all that and live your life as you please. Maybe you might need some help getting through the rough times. You'll have the memories and the nightmares.

If at times, it becomes overwhelming, I know of a counselor," she suggested.

"A counselor? Well, I don't know-" Shae hesitated. She wasn't crazy, at least she didn't think so.

"Just go once and if you don't feel it's helping, don't go back. I've been undergoing counseling for the past three years. I needed help dealing with everything that I experienced growing up. I feel that I really need it now, especially since I have my own children. I don't want to end up like her. I'd never want to mistreat, physically or mentally abuse my kids, ever!" Shae understood. "Just in case you change your mind, here's a card." She reached into her purse and handed Shae the business card she'd retrieved. "It really helps a lot," she ended.

"Thank you. I have to think about it."

"Well, take all the time you need."

They reached the park. Vivian brushed off a space on a bench and sat down.

"How are you coping right now?" Vivian questioned after Shae had taken a seat as well.

"I guess I'm doing okay. I just try not to think about it, that's all," she admitted.

"I know it's hard, but you are a very strong person. Not at all the scrawny little kid I remember," she said teasingly, and Shae smiled.

Vivian was so beautiful. She resembled the actress Vanessa Williams Fox. "I hated the way Mama treated you. I wish I could make it all go away, but I can't," Shae told her.

"You may never forget, but it'll get better in time." Vivian sighed. "I still have nightmares. You know, I told her about it," she said lowly.

"Told who, about what?"

Vivian stared off into the distance, her eyes vacant. "I told Mama about him raping me."

"Mama knew about Percy?" When Shae confronted her, Mrs. Byrts had reacted liked it was the first she'd heard of it.

Vivian nodded. "Yes. I told her everything, about how he used to come into the bathroom. I told about him touching me while I was asleep. I even told her how he was trying to molest you, too. That's when she started hitting me. She called me a liar and told me to shut up. She said there was no way that a man preferred a child when he could have a full-grown woman." She shook her head. "It devastated me that she didn't believe me. You'd think me being pregnant would be proof enough. I mean she never let us leave the apartment. How could I have gotten pregnant from anyone else?" She touched her cheek. "I had plastic surgery to cover the scars from that mirror incident," she revealed.

"Well, you're beautiful. You always were," Shae told her.

"Thank you." She smiled. "Once, I thought I'd be nothing without my looks. But, you know something? Looks aren't important at all. I learned that from a very special person."

"Oh? Who?" Shae asked.

"My husband, Richard." She leaned back on the bench and crossed her legs as she talked. "Rich used to be a fireman until he almost died saving a child from a burning building. He got burned pretty badly over most of his body. At first, I couldn't look past his physical appearance, but then I got to know him." She smiled lovingly. "He's wonderful and what's most important is that he's beautiful on the inside. I think you'll like Richard. He's a writer now."

189

"A writer? Really?" Shae asked, impressed.

"Yes. He writes mostly children's books and juvenile fiction. He's well paid for it, too," she said.

"That's great." Shae looked at Vivian. "So, what do you do besides work in that store?"

"That store happens to be mine," she said proudly. "I come in on the days that I'm not at the college campus."

"You go to college, too?" Shae asked in amazement. Vivian had her life together. She managed a family, ran a business, and attended college.

"Yes. I'm in my third year. Majoring in psychology. My minor is fashion marketing."

"That's wonderful! I wish I knew what I wanted to do," she said dully.

"You'll find yourself, eventually. You're still young," Vivian pointed out.

"You're talking like you're an old lady. You're only twenty-three," Shae reminded and Vivian laughed.

"Yes, you and Richard will love each other. He's always telling me that I'm wiser than my years. You've got to come over as soon as you get the chance," Vivian said, excited now.

"How many children do you have?" Shae asked remembering that her sister had mentioned kids. She couldn't believe that she was an aunt.

"Oh, I have twin girls. They're going through the "terrible twos." Their names are Rasheda and Rameyra. That brings me back to something. How are Charles and Chris now?" Vivian shook her head. "I still find it hard to believe that Mother tried to poison them," she said with bitterness.

190

"Yeah, me too," she replied. "They're doing good, though. Charles, for a while, they thought he wouldn't make it. But, he pulled through. DCF turned them over to Aunt Bea. They said I wasn't responsible enough to take care of them. At least, they didn't get sent some place where we couldn't see them."

"Things have a way of working out for the best. Maybe you'll get custody of the twins someday. Just keep the faith." She looked at her watch. "Oh my goodness! How time flies! I should at least tell Mrs. Ferguson to close up shop. I'll give you a lift home. That'll give me a chance to see Toby." They got up from the bench.

Shae was so happy that she'd found her sister. After so many years of being apart, it was a miracle to be together again. On in impulse, she threw her arms around her. Vivian seemed startled.

"What was that for?"

"Just to let you know, I love you," Shae said sincerely.

"I love you, too." Vivian said, hugging her back. "I've missed all of you. I just couldn't come back. I'm so sorry for deserting you."

Vivian felt the guilt eat away at her. Maybe if she'd kept in touch she could have saved Ma Violet. Ma Violet. Dear Ma Violet. She had been Vivian's lifeline back when she'd suffered from so much abuse. She'd run to Ma Violet when it got too bad to endure. Ma Violet always seemed to make things better. She'd calm the troubled waters, and Vivian would be able to go back home.

"You didn't desert us, Vivian," Shae said strongly. "Mama beat you almost every day. She might have killed you if you'd stayed. You had to

191

leave to save your life. Nobody blames you for leaving. Daddy may have deserted us, but you didn't!"

Shae remembered the night Vivian had left. She'd never forget trying to clean her sister's blood from the floor. She didn't fault Vivian at all. She'd done what she'd had to do in order to survive.

They went back to the store so that Vivian could get her purse and keys. She asked Mrs. Ferguson to lock up, said goodbye, and left.

Vivian drove a sleek Mercedes. Shae marveled at the leather interior.

"This is really nice," she said in admiration.

"Richard's gift to me for Mother's Day," Vivian told her proudly.

"Wow! Your husband buys you gifts like that? Must be nice!"

"You'll find your own Richard one day. Besides that horrible Dana, did you date anyone else?" She took her eyes off the road briefly to glance at Shae. "Whatever happened to that little boy who was always around? He had the prettiest eyes and was brown-skinned. If I can remember, he had a birthmark on his face."

"That's Larry," Shae said softly.

"Yes, that's his name. Whatever happened to him? You two made the cutest little couple. It was plain to see that he was completely smitten." Vivian chuckled.

"I lost my virginity to him," Shae shared.

"Oh my God! Really? That's a good thing, right?" Vivian glanced at her again then, back at the road.

"Yes. It was real special. Larry was- wow!" Shae could feel the heat rush to her face just from remembering.

192

"That good, huh?" They laughed.

"I miss him." Shae sighed. She hadn't realized just how much she actually did miss Larry until then. "He went off to college. I haven't heard from him since. He told me to keep in touch but with everything that's happened- well, I just haven't called." She didn't feel comfortable telling Vivian the details behind Larry's sudden departure.

"Things are looking up now. Maybe you should get in contact. Who knows, maybe the two of you can reconnect? Does thinking about him make your heart skip a beat?" her sister asked.

"Yes," she said and smiled fondly as she pictured Larry's face. It was a tender smile that Vivian didn't miss.

"That's how it is with Richard. Shae, you're in love, sweetheart!" Vivian explained. "You don't let a love like that slip away from you. You deserve happiness. Reach out and grab it, girl."

Vivian pulled up in front Shae's apartment, parked and shut off the engine.

"Who is that young, tender morsel?" Vivian asked. Shae noticed David mowing the yard. He had his shirt off, and the sweat falling from his body made his skin glisten.

"That's one of the landlord's sons. He has three of them, and they are all fine," she told her. Shae had seen all three and thought they resembled Chippendale models.

"Goodness! How can you stand it?" she asked as they got out.

"Vivian, I love Larry. I don't really pay much attention to anyone else."

193

"I may be married, but I have eyes. There's nothing wrong with looking," she stated as she closed the car door.

Shae waved at David, and he turned the lawn mower off.

"Hello beautiful ladies," he flirted.

"David, this is my sister, Vivian," Shae introduced.

"I see beauty runs in the family," he complimented. "Nice to meet you," he said to Vivian.

"And sexiness runs in yours," Vivian whispered low enough for only Shae to hear. She giggled.

"Thanks for mowing my yard," Shae said. "I thought I was supposed to do that."

"It's no big deal." David shrugged. "I don't mind helping out."

"It was nice meeting you, David," Vivian purred, wearing a big smile.

"Likewise," he replied and returned the smile. His smile made him look like a model on the cover of a fashion magazine. He restarted the mower and went back to cutting the grass.

"I think he might have a touch of jungle fever," Vivian told Shae as they went inside.

"He's just being nice."

"No one mows somebody's yard to be nice. That lil' Brad Pitt look-a-like has a crush on you. You sure you don't need a lil' *milk* for your coffee?" Shae laughed, happy to see that Vivian had a sense of humor. She hadn't turned out bitter because of all the abuse that had taken place in her childhood.

The two sisters sat and talked until it was time for Toby to arrive home from school. When he walked through the door, he didn't notice that they had company.

194

"Shae, my first day was tight!" he said with enthusiasm. "I already like this school. I don't think I'll be skipping none of my classes either," he told her then stopped and stared at Vivian. He didn't say anything, just stared.

"Toby, it's Vivian," Shae told him, excitedly.

"I- I know who she is," he finally said. Tears formed in his eyes, and he took a step forward but hesitated.

"Toby!" Vivian had tears in her own eyes. "Come here." She opened her arms and he rushed into them.

"Where did you go?" he choked out. "Why did you leave us?" The question wasn't an accusation. He only wanted to know. He'd been about eight years old the last time he saw his oldest sister.

"It's a long story." Vivian sighed. "Let's sit down and talk."

Shae made coffee for herself and her sister. Toby grabbed a soft drink from the refrigerator. Vivian told them about the night she'd left home for good. She ran off to Ma Violet's. Once Ma Violet took one look at her, she rushed her to the emergency room. She'd suffered a concussion and had three cracked ribs.

Once she recuperated, she went to a residential group home for runaway teenagers. That was where she began to put her life back together. After that, she went to a place called the Young Women's Residence, a long-termed shelter for abused girls. She got the opportunity to go back to school and to develop job skills. She'd also undergone months of individual and group counseling. She remained there until she turned eighteen.

She got hired as the clerk typist at the residential group home and was able to afford an efficiency apartment. She met Richard and fell in love. The rest, as the saying goes, was history.

CHAPTER TEN

Things fell into place for Shae. Her job was going well. Toby did a complete 180-degree turn-around. She'd gotten to meet her sister's husband and her nieces. She felt happy for the first time in her life.

At times, she found herself thinking about Larry and it would dampen her spirits. She couldn't forget the way things ended between them. She knew he'd left thinking the worst of her. After all, she'd told him she'd prostituted herself out to Dana. She wondered if he'd ever forgive her for lying to him.

She remembered the card he gave her the last day they'd been together. That was the awful day Dana had beaten her. It was also the day Charles and Chris almost died, and her mother had been arrested. The card was the only good thing that had came out of that day.

She searched through her box of keepsakes until she located it. Not knowing how Larry would react or if he'd even be at the number, she picked up the phone and dialed.

After she waited for the receptionist to connect her to the right room, a voice came on the line.

"Hello?" It didn't sound like Larry.

"Hello, is this Larry?" she inquired.

"No, wait a minute. I'll get him. Who's calling?"

"My name is Shae."

"Okay. Hold on a second."

"Hello?" Larry's voice sounded like music to Shae's ears.

"Hi, Larry. I was thinking about you, so I called," Shae said into the phone.

"Wait a minute, uh, who is this?" he asked, sounding confused.

"This is Shae. Shae Byrts from Florida. We grew up together. Remember?"

"Oh shit!" She heard the phone hit the floor. Seconds later, Larry got back on the line. "I'm sorry. It was just a shock. That fool Clarence told me it was someone named Cherika. Sweetheart, how have you been?" he asked thickly, overcome with emotion. He cleared his throat, recovered and laughed happily. "What's going on in ya life? Tell me everything. It's been so long."

Shae gave Larry a brief outline about what had happened after he'd left. "That's fucked up! You mean to tell me he actually tried to kill you?" he exclaimed when she relayed the part about Dana. "Baby, you've been through hell. I should have been there to watch out for you." They talked for quite a while. He updated her on his own life.

"I found out that there's a new art gallery right there in St. Pete and the owner is willing to promote my art. So, I'll be coming home. I was too eager to get away in the first place." He paused. "I never should have left you, Shae."

"That was my fault," she told him, remembering her lie.

"Aw- Shae. Let's not talk about that. All of that is in the past. I'm getting ready to move back to St. Pete." He hesitated, then said, "Maybe, if it's alright with you, we could pick up where we left off?" he asked gently. "I mean, if you ain't seeing someone, that is?" he added.

"There's no one," she told him.

Larry let out a relieved breath. "You know, I've been thinking about you constantly. I tried to forget you, but I just couldn't. I couldn't even force myself to date no one else," he revealed.

198

"You're just saying that."

"No, it's true, In spite of everything, I still love you. I'll never stop. Never."

"I couldn't get over you either," she told him. "That's why I called."

"I'm glad you did. Well, I better get off this phone. My roommate needs to use it. But, I'll see you in about two weeks," he told her. "The semester will be over, and I'll be coming home." She gave him her new address then they hung up.

Shae felt so excited. Suddenly, thoughts of how wonderful lovemaking had been with Larry filled her head. He had been her first love. Being with him had made her feel like she'd died and gone to heaven. Then, Dana raped her, and it had felt like she was in hell. She wondered if she'd ever again feel the way Larry had made her feel. Since Dana had taken a part of her that she could never get back, she felt that something was missing. It could only be replaced with a lot of patience and love. Would Larry have enough of either, or would he walk away after hearing the real reason she'd lied to him? Shae didn't want to risk losing him again, but knew she had to tell him the truth. She just didn't know when she'd tell him, but it was imperative that she did.

Vivian threw a cookout at her house in celebration of the family being together again. Shae had just finished braiding her hair into a French braid when she heard the doorbell. She answered the door and there stood Larry. It was totally unexpected. For a moment, she thought he was a figment of her imagination. She'd done nothing but think about him constantly since their phone conversation.

"Larry!" she squealed and threw her arms around him. His hard body symbolized he was indeed real.

"Wow! What a welcome home. Maybe I should leave more often," he joked.

"I missed you so much." She stood back to look him over. He had left a boy and returned a man. His features were more defined, and he had acquired muscles. As far as she was concerned, he was the best looking man she'd ever laid eyes on.

He held out a dozen, long stemmed, white roses. "Oh! Larry!" she gasped as tears formed in her eyes. No one had ever given her roses. Not even Dana with all of his money and fine jewels. Somehow, coming from Larry, the simple gesture had a magnitude of meaning.

"Can I kiss you?" he asked. Dear Larry. He was always the perfect gentleman. Shae turned her face up to his in eagerness. "God! How I've missed you," he groaned and crushed her to his chest. Their lips fused together. Shae felt her heart flutter. The magic hadn't disappeared. The question was, would it last once he found out that Dana had raped her?

"Larry, come on inside," she told him as she pulled away. "There's something I have to talk to you about." He came in and closed the door. "It's about what I told you concerning Dana." At the mention of that name, Larry's eyes slanted in anger.

"I don't want to hear about that. You did what you thought you had to do. Like I said over the phone, it's all in the past. Let it rest."

"But you don't understand. It wasn't like-"

"Shae, are you ready to go?" Toby asked as he entered the room. He looked really nice in casual attire. "Oh? I didn't know somebody was here. What's up, man?" he greeted Larry then did a double take. "Larry, man, where the hell have you been?" The two of them slapped hands then talked for a while until Shae reminded Toby that they had to go.

"Yeah, we better head out. I can't wait to beat Rich at chest again. Give me ten minutes," he said and left the room.

"Oh, y'all getting ready to go somewhere?" Larry asked.

"We're going to my sister Vivian's house for a family cookout. I'd like for you to come," she invited.

"No, I don't like to intrude on family matters."

"Larry, please," she begged. "I want you to be with me. Besides, Viv knows all about you. She remembers you as the skinny kid who had the crush on me."

"Well, if you really want me tagging along." He smiled gingerly.

"Of course I do. I want to spend every minute I can with you."

"That much time, huh?" He smiled again, showing even, white teeth. It caught Shae off guard at how handsome he'd become. His good looks made his birthmark fade into the background. She couldn't resist the urge to go into his arms again. They were kissing when Toby walked back into the room.

"If y'all finished locking lips, we can go. I can drive, if you want me to."

"Please! We want to arrive in one piece," Shae stated, putting the vase of beautiful roses in the center of the dining room table. She stood back and admired them. Larry smiled at the glow on her face.

"Those are some nice flowers," Toby stated as they headed out. "Larry, what are you trying to do, show all of us thugs up? Shoot, now, I'll have to step my game up." They walked down the stairs laughing.

Everyone in the family had been invited to Vivian's house. Aunt Beatrice brought her four children as well as Chris and Charles. Aunt Vernadine came along with two of her children, Tashae and Thomas. Shae introduced Larry to Vivian's husband Richard. They all sat around and talked as Vivian, Aunt Beatrice, and Aunt Vernadine went into the kitchen to help with the food. Some of the kids ran around the back yard playing tag. Others gathered around as Toby threw a football for them to catch.

"I'll be back. I'm going to help Viv and Aunt Bea in the kitchen," she told Larry and he nodded. He and Richard started discussing football. When Shae went inside she spotted her cousin Tashae.

"Girl, Larry has gotten too fine!" she complimented. "Are you two gonna finally get together?"

"I'm hoping that we do," Shae answered.

"If not, let me know. I'll be glad to take him off ya hands."

"No way, heifer! Not how you use and abuse men," Shae joked.

"Girl, you don't understand how it is. Once these niggas start trippin', I jus' have to diss 'em. Too many other men out there to cry over one. Right?" Shae just nodded. At one point in her life she had felt the same way, but things had changed. She couldn't imagine loving anyone else but Larry.

"Let me tell you about this fine ass nigga I met on the deuces," Tashae exclaimed. Shae shook her head at her cousin. They were the same age. Tashae had the same features, long hair and hazel eyes. Whereas Shae had begun to dress more conservatively, Tashae continued to wear short skirts and clingy tops that pulled attention to her body and good looks. Shae knew for a fact that her cousin was a cold-hearted bitch. She used to be just like her, and she was glad she'd changed.

Tashae rambled on and on about all the men she'd met at the clubs that she frequented. Shae smiled and pretended to be interested. She'd lost any excitement for partying and club hopping long ago. Dana had paraded her around so often that she'd begun to despise it. She doubted she'd ever frequent any of the hole-in-the-wall clubs that Tashae talked about ever again.

Shae picked up two plates and took them into the living room. The conversation had shifted to Mrs. Byrts. Shae glanced at Larry and noticed that he appeared to be uncomfortable.

"Want to go outside?" she suggested, setting the plates on a table.

"Yeah." He got up and followed her. They went through the sliding glass doors and closed them on the others.

"I'm sorry about that Larry," Shae apologized.

"It's okay," he assured. "It's not that I don't want to hear it, I do," he said quickly. "I just want to hear it from you, Shae."

"Where should I start?" she asked, taking a deep breath.

"From the beginning," he stated quietly.

She took a deep breath and let it out slowly. "Okay." She retold every horrible, gruesome moment of her life from the time Larry left. By the time she got to Dana surprising her in her family's home, she was crying.

"I hid some money at the apartment in the projects," she said between sniffles, "-so I went back to get it. Dana was waiting in the dark. He had a knife and he cut off all my hair. He sliced my face then stabbed me. I thought he was going to kill me." Larry pulled her into his arms. "He stabbed me Larry, over and over. I thought I was going to die!"

"It's okay. Just let it all out," he soothed. "I know it was hell holding it all inside, so just let it go." She cried for a long time, and he just held her. "I'm sorry Shae. You've been through so much. When you needed me, I wasn't around," he said with regret.

"You had to go away. Besides, I wouldn't let you get involved." She pulled back and wiped her eyes with the back of her hand. "Dana threatened to kill you. I didn't know what he was capable of. He might have done it. I didn't want to be responsible for that. So- so I lied to you about sleeping with him for money. I didn't do that." She hesitated. Since it was the moment of truth, she knew she couldn't keep her secret inside any longer. She went on. "Dana had Sly watching me. He saw us when we went to your house that night and he told him." She looked down. "Dana was mad because you and I slept together. He said you got what was supposed to be his. He beat me up, then- then he ra-"

"No, Shae! Don't tell me this!" Larry groaned.

"He raped me," she finished in a whisper.

204

"Please, don't say that." He took a step back. She tried to put her arms around him but he pushed her away.

"Larry, don't," she pleaded, staring into his stunned face.

"I can't deal with it, Shae. He had you? Like that? I can't handle this!" He shook his head from side to side. "I thought you were lying about sleeping with him for money. I figured you were just doing that to protect me. I never dreamed nothing like this. Man, you've been with him? That's fucked up!"

"Larry, how do you think I feel?" she asked in anguish.

"I- I don't know what to think. He *had* you," he said again in disbelief. "Shae, I'm sorry, but I just need some time to deal with this. I need to think."

"Larry." He backed further away then turned to leave. "Larry, don't go," she pleaded, but he wouldn't even look at her.

"I'll call a cab," he said and hurried back through the double doors; they closed with a click.

Shae sat in a plastic chair and tried to make sense of it all. She'd known Larry would handle it badly, but she hadn't expected for him to walk off and leave her. She'd thought about telling him and had fantasized how it would unfold. He'd be angry with Dana and would threaten to get even with him. He'd take her in his arms and tell her how sorry he was. He'd say over and over that it wasn't her fault; he still loved her, no matter what.

Reality crushed her spirits. She felt so empty inside, void of all emotions. Larry should have been the one person that would understand. Didn't he love her?

If he really cared, he wouldn't have reacted like that, her mind shrieked. *Wake up and face reality. Larry doesn't love you. He doesn't want someone who was used.*

She tried not to think about it, but the words kept reverberating inside her head. Her heart seemed to break into a thousand pieces. She'd never be so foolish as to fall in love again.

"Shae?" She looked up into Vivian's concerned face. "Shae, are you alright?"

"Yeah. I guess so," she lied.

"Come on inside and join the rest of us." Vivian could sense that something was wrong but she didn't pressure her sister. She'd seen Larry come back inside without Shae. Then he'd used the phone. As soon as the cab had pulled up, he'd left. "The men think they can beat us at Monopoly. So far, they're winning. We need you because Tashae just quit."

Shae let her sister talk her into going back inside and playing the game. After a while she forgot about Larry but only temporarily. She could never truly forget the greatest thing that had ever happened to her.

Shae sat outside, deep in thought. A shadow fell across the pages of a book that lay in her lap. Automatically, she tensed up thinking of Dana.

"Hey Shae. I thought that was you!" Memories from the past rushed back when she recognized Wade. She remembered the day she'd escaped from the Green Team. She'd never been so scared in her life. Wade had came back to help her. Wade had come- not Dana.

"Hello Wade," she greeted. "What's up?"

"Nothing much. I happened to be passing by and saw you sitting here, so I stopped. I ain't seen you in a long time." He paused. "I heard about what Dana did to you, and I'm real sorry." He shook his head. "I knew he was crazy, but I didn't know how crazy!" He paused. "So, how you holding up? You look good," he added, taking in her short haircut.

"Thanks," Shae replied. "I don't like to think about it much. I block it out for the most part. I just live day by day. I'm glad to be alive."

"I know what you mean." He glanced at her closely. "You still the prettiest woman I ever laid eyes one. I like your hair short, too," he added.

"Thank you," she said and smiled.

"So, er- uh, you hooked up with anybody? You got a man?" he asked.

"No." An image of Larry leaped into her head, but she dismissed it. "No one," she answered.

"Maybe we can go out sometime?" he offered.

"Well, I don't know," she hesitated.

"I know what you thinking," he said quickly. "And I want to tell you straight out, I'm not selling drugs anymore." He looked into her eyes. "I realized that I was jeopardizing my life, and I had no future. That ain't no way to live. I got out while I could."

"What do you do? I mean you just give up that kind of money. How do you, you know, what equals that?" she questioned.

"Nothing. You just have to compromise. Shae, money means nothing if you ain't happy. It's worthless if you scared shitless most of the time. What good is it?" She moved over and indicated that he could take a seat next to her on the step. He did. "Before I started that mess, I was on my way to college. Can you believe I blew a four-year scholarship because I was foolish enough to think there was an easy way out? I think about it a lot and regret the decision I made. I could have a degree in accounting or business management. I've wasted four years of my life."

"You wanted to be an accountant?" she asked and he nodded.

"Yeah. Believe it or not, I was smart once." He chuckled. "I made the honor roll every single grading period in high school! I just hated living in the projects, and I hated having my family live there. When I started selling drugs, the money was coming in fast. I got caught up in that and to hell with college. Why wait four years for a degree, which ain't even no guarantee that you'll get a job when you get it? That's the way I used to think. But now- I'm back to my right frame of mind. You know what changed me?"

"What?"

"A chickenhead." Shae's eyes widened. His story was intriguing. "Man, this girl used to be so fine!" He went on. "I mean, I went to school with her, and she won beauty contests and everything. Somehow, she got hooked on crystal meth and crack. When she approached me, I didn't even recognize her. She looked jacked up! She was all skinny and dried up! And when she looked in my eyes and asked me if I remembered her, I was like, "You joking, right?" And she said, "Nah, I'm Jennifer Stevens. We went to Northeast High and graduated in the same class." I was shocked! I couldn't believe it. What really got to me though was, she didn't have enough money for the drugs, and she offered to sleep with me. I told her no but she kept begging. I mean she was desperate. It tore me up on the inside," he admitted.

208

"It just did something to me. I actually had tears in my eyes. I just shook my head and gave her the crack. After that, I couldn't sell drugs again."

"That's sad," Shae told him. "Drugs are so addicting."

"Yeah, they are."

"I'm glad you got out of the game."

"I'm glad, too. I don't want to contribute to that kind of destruction of my own people. It's selfish." A horn blew and he looked up. "My lil' brother is getting impatient. He's waiting for me in the car. I'm taking him to the zoo." He looked at her. "Hey, you want to come?" he asked. "That is, if you don't have anything else planned." Shae looked into his face. All she saw was kindness.

"I've never been to the zoo," she told him. "I'd be glad to come."

They walked to his car together, and he introduced her to his seven-year-old brother, Cortez.

Shae never expected to actually have fun looking at animals, but she did. She was actually more excited than Cortez. Wade bought them popcorn, cotton candy, and balloons. She hadn't had cotton candy since she was a little girl, and it brought back happier times. She remembered when her father had taken her and Vivian to the state fair. They rode all the rides and had fun trying to win the different prizes. Before they left the fairgrounds, he bought both of them candy apples and a huge bag of different colored cotton candy. She smiled as she reminisced.

"I can see by the smile on your face that you're happy," Wade commented as he got his keys and unlocked the car.

"Yes, I am." She smiled. She looked down at Cortez who staggered sleepily. "I think he's worn out." Wade opened the back door and picked Cortez up. He settled him in the back seat where he immediately drifted off.

"So, you had a good time?" he asked and Shae nodded. "Maybe we can go out again soon- without Tez?" he suggested.

"I'd like that. Call me and let me know." He handed her his cell phone and she stored her number in it.

They listened to a soft jazz station as he drove in the direction of her house. It wasn't long before Wade pulled up in front of her apartment.

"I will call. You can believe that." He smiled at Shae with admiration and gave her a chaste kiss on the cheek. She got out and waved goodbye.

"Tell Cortez I really enjoyed hanging out with him," she told Wade.

"What about hanging with me?" he teased.

"I enjoyed your company, too. Thank you," she said. Wade watched until she was safely inside her apartment. Then he pulled off.

Shae dated Wade for a few weeks, but her heart wasn't in it. She found herself constantly thinking about Larry, wondering if he'd call. She missed him so much that it hurt. She didn't feel right leading Wade on. He genuinely was a nice guy. Since she didn't want him to think there would be more to their relationship, she broke it off.

They'd just returned from the movies. Shae let Wade come inside, and the gesture made him think that something more would take place. Shae put a quick end to that thought.

"Wade, we need to talk." She pushed against his chest when he reached for her.

"Okay." He noticed that she'd moved over, putting some distance between them on the couch. That wasn't a good sign.

"I know that you have some feelings for me-" she began.

"Yeah, I have strong feelings for you," he interrupted. "I really care about you."

Shae sighed. "That's why I need to talk to you. You may want a relationship with me, Wade, but I don't feel the same way," she said gently. "I think it's best that we don't see each other anymore."

"Aw Shae." Wade groaned. "Is it somebody else?" He stared into her eyes.

"Yes," she answered in honesty.

"It's that other guy, right? The one before Dana?" She nodded. "Are you in love with him?"

"Yes. I am. I'm in love him," Shae admitted, which caused Wade's face to fall. "I'm sorry."

"Don't apologize. You can't force yourself to feel something that you don't." He shook his head in regret. "I knew it. I could feel you holding back. You were with me, yet you weren't." He sighed deeply. "Well, I hope he makes you happy." He kissed her gently on the lips and got up, dejected. Shae hated hurting him, but her heart belonged to Larry, and it always would.

CHAPTER ELEVEN

S hae threw herself into her work in an effort to dull the ache in her heart. After six months, she got a raise for being such a dedicated employee at the bank. Her manager informed her of a program that helped people receive their GED, so she enrolled in the class.

Mrs. Watson had glimpsed the potential the first time she'd encountered Shae Byrts. It was uncommon for them to hire someone who significantly lacked education. But, she'd felt that the young woman had what it took to become a great asset to the Union First Bank if given a chance. She'd been right.

For a while, she'd sensed a deep sadness in the girl and it tugged at her heart. The story of what her mother had done had been plastered in the headlines for weeks. There wasn't anyway she could have not known, but she wasn't one to pry into people's personal affairs. If and when Shae wanted to talk, her door would be open.

After everything the young girl had experienced, she wanted to do something to give her proof that her life could be turned around. She just couldn't give up. And Shae had already proven that she was a fighter.

How many people could rise above a life of poverty and abuse, survive a stabbing, and deal with the horror and shame of her mother's incarceration? Yet, Shae had endured and she'd persevered.

In spite of everything that had happened, Shae remained an exemplary employee. She came to work daily and on time. She was a team player who never complained about the strenuous workload. She even stayed well past five o'clock some nights when they were short staffed, even on Fridays.

When she'd suggested that Shae further her education, she could see the light behind her eyes shine with renewed hope. Giving someone a chance was the Godly thing to do and Mrs. Watson was all about honoring Him. She felt truly blessed and was only too glad to become a blessing to someone else. It was her Christian duty, and she knew that it would be pleasing in the sight of God.

Since being so busy, Shae didn't have much time to dwell on the past. On occasion, she'd catch herself thinking about how life could have turned out if things had been different. At that point, none of the things she'd thought so important seemed to matter. She didn't care about fancy cars, money, clothes, or jewelry. She wasn't even concerned with her looks. She came to the realization that just as God had given her looks, He could also snatch them away.

Her hair had almost grown to its regular length. She realized that she actually liked it better shorter. She found a hairstyle in *Black Hair* magazine that fit her and got it cut. With a bob, she looked professional and classy. After coming so close to death, she'd grown to appreciate the simple things life had to offer. She now knew how to, as Ma Violet used to say: *take time out and smell the roses!*

She truly missed Larry and wanted to get in touch with him. The thought of being rejected again held her back. Loving Larry and not being able to have him caused a constant ache in her heart.

213

She remembered the night he walked off when she told him about being raped. It had hurt her to the core of her being. Larry, her best friend, hadn't been able to understand. He couldn't deal with the idea of her having been with another man, even if it had been by force. She didn't know how she'd do it, but she had to make a life for herself. It would be one filled with happiness because she deserved it. She'd have that life, even if it meant having it without Larry.

She would work hard and eventually that hard work would pay off. She'd already received a raise. Her manager had informed her about GED certification offered at Pinellas Technical Education Center. She enrolled in their night classes and only had three more weeks left before she received her GED. Once she obtained that, she would try to get promoted to head teller. She might even consider furthering her education by going on to college. She'd purchased a computer and could even take online classes at St. Petersburg College. There were so many possibilities. She wouldn't stop living because Larry didn't want her. She'd find someone who could love her in spite of her flaws and imperfections. Even so, that didn't stop her from missing him.

"Shae, you've done a fine job all week," Mrs. Watson told her. "You can pull your till and count it. Then, go on home." She winked and leaned close enough for only Shae to hear. "We'll pretend it's five o'clock," she whispered.

"Thank you, Mrs. Watson." Shae smiled her gratitude. She hadn't expected that. Sure, Mrs. Watson was nice, but she never showed favoritism toward any of her employees. Shae felt lucky as she counted her register drawer. Meeting Mrs. Watson had been a blessing.

"Don't forget to pick up your check," Charnell told her as she headed out. "You may need it."

"I sure do. Thanks for reminding me," Shae told the other girl. Charnell was a sweet, quiet girl who rarely spoke unless spoken to.

"Have a nice weekend," Charnell called as she left.

"You, too. Bye."

At home, she checked the mailbox. She expected magazines, bills and junk mail. It thrilled her to see a letter addressed from James Wallace on one of the envelopes. She opened it quickly and read what he had to say.

Dear Shae,

What's up, girl? It's like, hey! I'm sorry for the way we parted. I was under a lot of pressure. You know how it is.

Anyway, how have things been going? What's Toby up to and how are the twins? Have you seen Larry lately? Tell my nigga I said, "What up?"

The Army is okay. I've finished basic training and am stationed at Camp Pendleton in California. Like I said, things are okay. The only thing I'm worried about is that I may get sent overseas to Iraq. I really don't want to go there, and a lot of my buddies feel the same way. I think if I go overseas- I may never come back. It's really strange, but I keep having these nightmares. It's weird. I just don't want to go to Iraq, I know that much. But, let me not burden you with all that.

Well, as you know, I'm not much of a writer. If you answer my letter, I will continue to send a reply. I'm really going to need a lot of support, especially if I have to go over there. Don't think of me as a coward. I know what I got myself into when I enlisted. To die for oil- I'm not sure it's worth it. But, I'll fight for my country until the end.
Well, I'll close this letter but not my love. (Nigga always wanted to say that.) Ha! Ha! See ya!

Sincerely yours,

James L. Wallace

PS: Send me some pictures. I'm sick of looking at all these dried up ass hoes here in Cali!

Shae finished reading the letter and laughed aloud. Hearing from James made her feel good inside. It impressed her that he wanted a better way of life. He was finally growing up. The Army would help to mold him. She understood his apprehension about going to Iraq. Anyone would feel the same way.

She sat down and wrote him back. She included a condensed version of what had happened to Ma Violet, the twins, and her close call with death. She dug out some pictures that she'd taken in the clubs she used to frequent. She put those inside the envelope with the letter, sealed it then walked to the mailbox located a block away.

"Hi Shae!" She glanced up after putting the letter in the mailbox and saw her co-worker, Charnell. Shae waved at her then froze. The car that Charnell sat in looked familiar. She walked up to the passenger's side.

"Charnell, this is a bad ride," she said casually. "Who do it belong to?"

"It's y new friend's car. He's so sweet." Charnell blushed and giggled.

"Oh, really? What's his name?"

"Dana." Shae stepped back as if she'd been slapped. She'd had a suspicion that the car belonged to him but had hoped she was wrong.

"What's the matter?" the naïve, young girl looked closely at Shae.

"I have to tell you something, and I hope you don't take it the wrong way." She hurried to relay the story of what Dana had done to her. Once she finished, Charnell sat back in shock. "Get away from him as soon as you can. He is trouble, and he's ruthless," Shae warned. "The last thing I'd want is to see you hurt, Charnell. You're such a sweet person."

"I'm sorry you went through all that, Shae. I had no idea that Dana was that kind of person. I just met him," she said. "I will definitely take your advice to heart. I don't need that type of drama in my life. I have two kids, and I can't risk them seeing their mama being abused."

"No one deserves that," Shae agreed.

Charnell glanced around nervously. "I guess you should hurry up and leave before he comes back. I don't want him to see us talking. Thank you so much for telling me."

"Take care."

"You, too."

"See you at work."

"See you."

PROJECT QUEEN

On the way back to the apartment, scenes of what Dana had done to her kept resurfacing. Shae couldn't believe that he'd gotten out of jail already. He'd almost killed her, and he now walked free. That wasn't right.

"Hello." Shae jumped at the sound of a male's voice.

"Oh, hello." She breathed a sigh of relief when she saw David.

"I didn't mean to startle you," he apologized. "I've got some bad news, but don't get alarmed," he rushed on to say.

"What? Is it my brother?" Fear leapt in her throat.

"No. He's fine, as far as I know," David assured her. "The problem is, someone tried to break into your apartment. I came to put up the ceiling fans and caught him before he could get in."

"Damn!"

"If you need anything or you feel unsafe, I can stay with you," he offered. "We can call my dad or the cops," David offered.

"That's alright. My brother will be here soon. Thanks for offering."

"No problem. You take care."

"Thanks."

Shae hurried upstairs and unlocked the door. Once inside, she checked all the windows. Still, she didn't feel safe. She kept thinking about Dana. Knowing that he'd been released from jail made her nervous and scared. If they met up again, he'd finish what he'd started. She felt positive about that. He really hated her because she reminded him of his mother. His warped mind had him convinced that Shae deserved the same fate as his mama.

She paced the floor and prayed that Toby would get there soon. The shrill ringing of the phone in the quietness of the apartment made her jump.

"H- hello?" she answered.

"Shae?" The voice sounded hesitant.

"Yes?"

"Uh...this is Larry." He paused. "So, how have you been?"

"I've been okay. How about you?" Again, there was a long moment of silence. Then he blurted out the truth.

"I've been going through pure hell! Spending these last few months without you has been crucial. I was a damn fool. Shae, can you ever forgive me for the way I acted?" he asked. The conversation brought up past hurts that Shae thought she'd buried. She took a deep breath.

"I forgive you, but I want you to know that you really hurt me bad, Larry. I needed for you to understand. You didn't."

"I know. I know. I've been an asshole! I thought about it all over and over. I should have handled it in a different way. Can we give it another try? I miss you like crazy."

"I miss you, too. We need to sit down and discuss it face-toface. But...Larry, I have to tell you something."

"What is it?" he asked quickly, hearing the alarm in her voice.

"He's out. Dana. He's out of jail – and I'm scared," she almost whispered.

"You don't have to be scared. If Dana ever fucks with you, he's as good as dead! That's a promise," he said, and she believed him.

"Someone tried to break into the apartment today," she went on hurriedly. "I thought maybe it was him or one of his people. Maybe he found out where I live and-"

"Shae, calm down. Is Toby there?"

"No."

"You're alone?" he exploded.

"Yes."

"Don't worry about nothing. I'll be there in fifteen minutes. No, make that ten. Don't answer the door for no reason until I get there, you hear?" he instructed.

"Okay. Bye." She hung up, feeling relieved. Larry would be there shortly. She knew she could count on him.

True to his word, Larry got there in ten minutes flat. Shae peered through the eyehole. Seeing him, she opened the door and rushed into his arms.

"I'm so glad you're here," she exclaimed.

"You don't have to worry now." He took her face in his hands and gazed into her eyes. "I love you, Shae. I always will."

"I love you, too, Larry," she answered and turned her willing lips up to meet his.

"Cut out that mushy stuff." Toby's voice startled them and they broke apart.

"Toby," Shae exclaimed. "Don't be scaring people like that!"

"What's up?" he asked, hearing the fear in her voice. He came in and closed the door. He carried a bag from Big Tim's Barbeque that he sat on the kitchen table. When Shae told him about the earlier incident, he frowned. When she mentioned that Dana had got out of jail, his face reflected pure hatred.

220

"Shit! We have a fucked up judicial system!" he cursed. "What are we supposed to do, just hide out like some scared ass wimps? Hell nah! I ain't with that! Dana don't scare me. I'll fuck that nigga up, if I have to," he said. He pushed away from the table angrily and left the room.

In his bedroom, he got down on his knees and looked under the bed. He pulled the shoebox out and lifted the lid. He got the gun and placed it in the pocket of his jacket. When he came from his room, he appeared calm.

"I'll be back," he told Shae. "Look after my sister," he said to Larry in a strange voice. Larry nodded. He picked up on the glint in Toby's eyes. It was a look that should put fear in someone's heart.

"What are you going to do Toby? Maybe you should just stay-" Shae began.

"Don't worry," he interrupted. "I'm going to do what I have to." He went to the door, paused, and turned around. He stared at them both then walked out.

Shae sat down on the couch because her legs almost gave out.

"Are you okay?" Larry asked.

"I'm alright. It's just that, I wonder why all of this is happening. All I want is to be able to live my life. That's all."

"Don't worry about it, Shae. Dana knows the consequences he'll face if he harasses you or anybody in your family. I'm sure he don't want to go to prison."

"I don't think he cares about that. When will it end?" she questioned. "I just want it all to stop."

"Don't upset yourself." He sat down and put his arms around her. "Forget about it for now. Let's

221

concentrate on each other." He leaned in and kissed her. "Just relax and let me love you."

He trailed gentle kisses down her neck. He unbuttoned her blouse and touched her breasts. She trembled. "It's okay," he whispered. "It's me." He finished undressing her and kissed every inch of her body. Soon, she forgot everything around her except him and his delicious touch. Passion overcame her. She wrapped her legs around his waist as he entered her.

"I've missed you, baby," he groaned as they became one.

The horrible visions of Dana raping her were washed away. All she could feel was Larry inside her and Larry loving her. It had taken him to mend her heart and to heal her soul. He was the missing piece of her puzzle. Now she felt complete.

Afterwards they lay entwined on the couch. She felt happier than she had in a long time. She rested her head against his strong shoulder. Maybe there could be a happily ever after for her.

"You're mine, Shae, and I won't let anyone ever hurt you. I promise," Larry told her. Their lips met. "I'm a part of your life, and I'll never leave you again. Do you believe me?"

"Yes." She gently touched his cheek. He meant the world to her. "Let's go to my room," Shae suggested, straightening her clothes. "Toby might walk in on us." The two got up. As they headed for the bedroom, loud gunshots interrupted the stillness of the night. An agonizing scream rang out.

"Oh God! Toby!" Without thinking, Shae ran to the door and snatched it open. Larry's first instinct was to follow her, but he had to catch Dana off guard. He quickly slipped into the bedroom. He grabbed the revolver he'd brought with him. He would wait for the right moment. He knew that Dana would show up because he knew how a twisted mind operated. Dana was obsessed with Shae. If he couldn't have her, then he wouldn't let anybody else have her either.

Larry was prepared for the event and Dana would feel his wrath. Shae had belonged to him first, and if Dana hadn't forced himself on her, she would have belonged to him only.

The thought of Dana violating his woman made his blood run cold. One of them would leave the apartment standing and one would leave in a body bag. He was certain of that.

He heard Dana's voice and had to restrain himself from rushing out the bedroom blasting. He had to be patient and wait. Shae's life was at stake and he'd be damned if he was going to lose her.

"Just the person I want to see." Dana stood in the doorway with a gun aimed at Shae. He smiled, showing his sparkling, gold-plated grill.

"What happened to my brother?" she demanded to know.

"Don't worry 'bout it, bitch!" he snarled. "The fucking snitch got what he deserved. He got away this time, but he won't be so lucky the next time." He pushed past her and entered the apartment. Two other men followed him. They were dressed in all black and wore hooded sweatshirts. Shae recognized one of them as Sly, the neighborhood snitch.

"What the fuck you starin' at?" he snapped, glaring at her through bloodshot eyes. She remembered that he'd been the one to tell Dana about her and Larry. Shae wanted to claw his eyes out but held back.

"You and me got a score to settle," Dana growled. "I should have stopped ya ass when I had the chance, but I actually cared about you."

"That's a lie! All you care about is yourself."

"Bitch, you sellin' out to the wrong nigga!" The guy she didn't know warned. "Dana, I'll be glad to pistol whip this bitch for you. Just say the word!" He glared at her with his lips curled, waiting for instructions.

"That's okay. I can handle her. Y'all two go try to find that coward," Dana ordered. "This time, shut him up for good. Bury his weak ass. I'll be damned if I go back to jail for any nigga!" he snarled. "I got some business to take care of." His eyes swept over Shae's body suggestively. The two guys smirked, nodded at him and left.

Dana locked the door then turned to Shae. "I think it's time we got reacquainted. I missed you, in a way." He grabbed her by the shoulder in a painful grip. "You know what to do."

Shae felt the hatred pulse through her blood. She pursed her lips and spat directly into his vile face. She remembered Larry and his promise. She trusted that he'd do what he said he would.

"You no good bitch!" Dana yelled and slapped her across the face. He drew his arm back to strike her again, but Larry appeared. "I'm gonna fuck you up."

"I wouldn't do that," Larry warned, and Dana whirled around to face him. He was caught completely off guard. The two men faced off.

Shae took the opportunity to bring her knee up into Dana's groin. He moaned in pain and dropped his gun. It skittered across the floor and she grabbed it. She wanted to blow him away right then and there, but Larry took over.

"No, Shae. I won't let you go to jail for this motherfucker! Your brothers need you. Give me the gun," he urged.

"But if I don't do something, he's going to kill me," she sobbed.

"Trust me, Shae. Didn't I tell you that I wouldn't let that happen? I promised you that I wouldn't let nobody hurt you ever again. Give me the gun. Please."

Dana pulled himself together, but he still held his privates as he swore.

Shae looked directly into Larry's eyes. "Give it to me," he coaxed. With reluctance, she handed it over. He took the gun and placed it on the coffee table. Then, he took his own revolver and pointed at Dana.

Dana's eyes opened wide in disbelief. "No man! Please! Don't do it!" he begged. "I ain't never did nothin' to you!"

"You hurt my lady! Raped my lady, bitch! You think that's nothing?" Maybe he wouldn't kill him. He could just shoot him in the kneecap. It took a cold-hearted person to take someone's life. He didn't know if he could be that type of person.

Dana saw the doubt in Larry's eyes and it gave him courage. He was dealing with another softy. "That bitch needed me to fuck her," he said, suddenly bold. "Ya bitch ass wasn't hitting it right. You 'bout a punk ass motherfucker! You aiming that gun, but you too chickenhearted to pull the trigger, fuckass nigga!" He laughed and pulled himself up off the floor. "Tell me something. What did it taste like?" he asked.

"What?" Larry's hand shook as he aimed.

"My jism, nigga? What did it taste like? I skeeted all up in ya bitch the last time I fucked her! It's like my dick slid down ya throat and my nuts rested on ya chin while I nutted in ya mouth."

"What the fu-!" A red haze suddenly clouded his vision. He felt the trigger on the gun move. Larry fired one shot that hit Dana right between the eyes. Blood splattered everywhere as the back of his head exploded. Dana toppled over and hit the floor with a heavy thud. He shook, took a deep, gulping breath then died. His evil eyes stared at them.

"See, didn't I tell you to trust me?" Larry asked Shae. "He'll never hurt you again." They both stared at Dana's lifeless body.

"You killed him." Shae stated the obvious.

"We'll say it was in self-defense," he said in a calm voice. Shae was amazed at how calm Larry was. "He tried to break in and we thought it was the burglar who was here earlier."

The phone rang and Shae automatically answered it. Toby was calling to check on them and to let her know that he was fine. The police had apprehended the two guys chasing him. He'd been grazed in the leg but only suffered a flesh wound. He was getting patched up at the ER as he talked.

"Dana's dead," she said into the receiver. She could hear him breathe a great sigh of relief. "I know you're tired of running," she stated. "It's all over now. We can finally live in peace."

The police pounded on the door just as Shae hung up the phone. Larry went to answer. She would leave it up to him to take care of things. She gazed over at Dana and felt no remorse or guilt. Was it wrong for her to feel relieved? Dana had brought it upon himself. Bad karma always comes back

around. We reap what we sow. And as Ma Violet
used to say, *God don't like ugly.*

CHAPTER TWELVE

Larry's version of the events leading to Dana's death was accepted as the truth. No one cared about what had really happened to Dana except maybe his relatives. The two men involved, Sly and Willie, pleaded guilty to attempted murder. They'd be behind bars for a long time. Toby's wounds healed and he went back to school. Everyone had adjusted and moved forward with their lives except for Shae.

She kept having nightmares. She'd wake up screaming in the middle of the night. She couldn't sleep alone, so Larry moved in with them. She started crying for no reason and couldn't explain why. She had turned into an emotional wreck. She feared that maybe she was going insane like her mother.

Larry didn't know what to do. He tried to be supportive and understanding. His own nerves were shot. He finally made a suggestion.

"Shae, you got to pull it together," he told her one morning after he found her crying into her plate of food. "You are stronger than this. Don't let it break you. If you fall apart, all of it- everything would have been for nothing. Dana's death would be for nothing." She continued to cry, not able to stop. "Please. I hate seeing you like this." He licked his lips nervously. "Maybe you should talk to someone. Maybe that would help."

"If that's what you want," she managed to say between sobs. "I don't know what's wrong with me," she said, wiping at her tears.

"Will you do it? Will you go talk to someone about how you feel? I don't know what to do. I'm not a professional."

"I'm willing to do anything. Anything. I just want to be like I used to be. Just don't leave me, Larry. I need you."

"I'm not going no where, baby. I'm in it for the long haul." After everything we've been through, please know that."

She nodded and whispered, "I know."

"I just want you back."

Shae found the card that Vivian gave her months ago. She called the number and set up an appointment with a counselor. She felt better just by doing that. She'd taken the first step.

The first time she talked to the counselor, they focused on her unhappy childhood. She vented her frustration about being deserted by her father, having to care for her younger siblings, and being constantly belittled and both physically and mentally abused by her mother. She got to let out the anger she felt, the resentment, and the hatred. She voiced her fears about thinking she'd become like her mother.

The counselor was very attentive and non-judgmental. They ended the session by dealing with self-esteem issues and anger management. Shae discovered that it was okay to be angry. It was okay to feel confused. She had a renewed hope and left feeling that things would only get better.

After a few more sessions with her counselor, she could talk openly about her mother and how she felt. She found that she wanted her mother's approval, even her love. She would forgive her for the abuse, but she couldn't forget about her poisoning the twins or killing Ma Violet. She didn't know if she'd ever be able to forgive any of it. Only God could forgive certain sins.

***

"Shae, I thought you said that counseling was helping you?" Toby questioned.

"It is. Why?" She turned to look at him.

"You don't look so good," he told her. "Hell, you look tore up from the floor up!"

"Thanks," she said sarcastically. "I just feel nauseous. Sick to my stomach."

"Oh, maybe it's the flu. Ma Violet used to always fix lemon tea with honey. It worked." He looked in the refrigerator and rummaged around. "We don't have lemons, but I'll go to the store and get some."

"Thanks, Toby. I guess I'll go lie down for a while."

"I'll be back with the lemons," he told her getting the keys off the dresser. Shae had applied for an automobile loan from the bank and had been approved. She now owned a new Toyota Corolla.

She headed to her bedroom but had to take a detour to the bathroom. She felt the bile rush up to her throat. She leaned over the toilet for fifteen minutes and vomited. When she finished, she felt weak and tired.

"Shae, I'm back!" She heard Toby call out. Seconds later, he peered into the bathroom because she'd left the door open. "It's probably a stomach virus," he stated. "I think you should see a doctor."

"Can you call Vivian? I'm too weak to go anywhere. Help me to my room," she said.

230

Toby called Vivian, and she came right away. When she took one look at Shae, she called her family physician, Dr. McNeil, who made home visits. Since he couldn't make it until the following day, Vivian stayed over to look after her.

Both Vivian and Toby watched over her like two mother hens. They forced her to eat chicken soup and drink hot, lemon tea. Toby wanted to call Larry at work but Shae wouldn't hear of it.

"I'm fine. I don't want him to stop working because he's worried about me." Larry often worked late at the studio. On occasion, he could get creative and paint well into the night. His creations were beautiful, and he couldn't paint fast enough to keep up with the demand for his work.

When he got home and found her in the bed, he took over.

"They should have called me," he said worriedly. "Are you alright? How you feel, baby?" he asked, touching her forehead.

"Okay," she mumbled. "I'm feeling much better now that you're here."

He grinned from the compliment. "You feel like eating something?"

"Oh no. Viv and Toby stuffed me with chicken soup. I can't eat another bite."

"Dr. McNeil will be here in a little while," Vivian informed. "One of his patients cancelled, so he can come after all."

"I'm going to let you get some rest. Okay? Get better, baby." He leaned down and kissed her gently on the lips.

"Larry, if I have the flu, you're going to catch it," she warned.

"What a better way!" He laughed then grew serious. "I love you. Hurry up and get well. I have something important to ask you."

Dr. McNeil, a short, robust man with a smiling, jovial face came. His hearty laugh was infectious. He entered the room carrying his black, doctor's bag.

"Well, Miss Lady, let's see what we have here." It didn't take long for him to look her over. "When was your last cycle?" he asked. Shae couldn't remember.

"I don't know. I guess it's regular. But, well-" Now that it had been brought to her attention, she hadn't had a menstrual cycle in over a month and a half. "It's late," she admitted.

"Well, in that case, don't seem to be anything wrong with you that nine months won't cure," he said, and smiled. It took a while for his statement to register in her brain.

"What do you mean?" she asked.

"Well, young lady. I can be almost certain that you're expecting."

"Expecting what? A baby?" It hadn't dawned on her that pregnancy could be a possibility. "I guess I'm glad it's not the flu."

"That young man you got will be mighty proud. He should be," Dr. McNeil added. "If you need me at any time, just call, you hear?"

"Thank you Dr. McNeil." Shae watched him leave.

Larry, Vivian, and Toby rushed into the room.

"Well, what's wrong?" Vivian asked. "Is it the flu?" she wanted to know.

"It's a stomach virus. Right?" Toby questioned. Larry said nothing just stared at her with concern.

"There's nothing wrong. I'm just going to have a baby," she told them.

"So, in other words, that means you're okay?" Toby said. "Wait a minute! Did you say you having a baby?"

"Shae, this is wonderful!" Vivian went to her sister's side. "I'm pregnant again too!" They hugged in excitement. Larry appeared to be in a daze.

"So- I'm gonna be a father? Right?" he finally managed to get out. They all laughed. "I'm gonna be a daddy! Whooooo Weeeeee!" He jumped up in the air. "I wanted to ask you something as soon as you were well, but I guess you ain't really sick. Anyway, I can't hold it in no more." He approached the bed and took her hand in his. "I love you and I would be honored if you'd marry me." He gazed into her eyes then got down on one knee. "Shae Byrts, will you be my wife?" Tears filled her eyes.

"Yes," she whispered.

"I don't have an engagement ring right now. It's still on lay-a-way at K-Mart." He stared at her in mock seriousness then burst out laughing. "That was a joke. It's like, y'all can laugh now." No one did.

"Larry, you an okay kinda guy," Toby told him. "But, don't quit ya day job!" They all laughed. Happiness surrounded the room and embraced everyone in it.

Over the next few weeks, both Larry and Shae were excited about the pregnancy. Shae and Vivian had already gone shopping several times for baby clothes. Babies could never get enough pampers, baby wipes and toiletries.

Shae had just returned from the mall when Larry came home.

"What are you doing home so early?"

"I'm on a mission," he said mysteriously. "I have something to show you. Come on." He grabbed her hand.

"Where are you taking me?"

"Just come on," he said, excitedly. Shae felt like a kid a Christmas time as she let him lead her to the car.

Minutes later they pulled up in front of a magnificent two-story, brick home. It resembled a real-life dollhouse. They got out and She stared in awe.

"Who lives here?" she asked.

Larry, smiling, took her hand. "We do." Shae couldn't contain herself, and started to jump up and down in her excitement. "Hey, hey!" Larry cautioned. "Don't shake up the baby. Calm down." He fondly rubbed her slightly protruding stomach.

"Larry, for real? Is this really our house?"

"Yes. Well, it will be as soon as we sign the paperwork. I just wanted to make sure that you liked it first," he told her.

"I love it."

"But you haven't even seen the inside."

"I still love it."

"There are four bedrooms. So Toby can have his own room. Charles and Chris can share a room, one can be a nursery and of course, we get the master bedroom."

"Oh Larry. You mean it? You don't mind that my brothers will be living with us? You know Aunt Bea will let them live with-"

"Shh!" He put his finger up to her lips to silence her. "I won't hear of it." Larry gave her a firm look. "Shae, after the life you and your brothers went through, what kind of a person would it make me if I didn't do all I could to keep y'all together? Those are your brothers- your family. Family is the most important thing in the world to me. And a family belongs together." He took her hands in his and stared deeply into her eyes. "I love you," he said thickly. "That means I love your brothers just like they're my brothers. As your future husband, I'm just as responsible for them as you are." He squeezed her hand reassuringly. "Now, come on. I want you to see inside of our new home."

"Larry, you are something else," she said quietly as they walked up the driveway.

"I'm glad you think so. I remember when we first met. You called me stupid." Shae gave him a puzzled look then after a moment she burst into laughter.

"Even then, you were something else." She smiled. "You gave me a Band Aid for my scraped knee. That was so sweet."

"Even back then, I knew how to woo the ladies. I was just enduring you to me forever," he joked.

"Well, it worked."

Larry opened the door and held it for Shae. When she stepped inside, she gasped in surprise. A trail of rose petals led to the dining room. There on the table set a romantic dinner for two. The sparkling candles couldn't outshine the sparkle in Shae's gaze.

"Oh Larry," she exclaimed. "This is beautiful!"

"You're beautiful. Now, I know I already asked you to marry me, but I didn't have the ring." He reached in his pocket and pulled out a jewelry box. "Now that I have the engagement ring, I'd like to pose the question all over again. Shae, will you marry me?"

He opened the ring box and a two-carat diamond glistened and flashed at her.

"Wow! It's so beautiful."

Larry cleared his throat. "Is that a yes or a no?"

"Stop teasing! Yes, I'll marry you. I love you."

"I love you, too." He took the ring from the box and slid it onto her finger. "I like the look of that." He nodded proudly.

"It's perfect." She took in the wonderful candlelit dinner. "You did all this for me?" She hugged him around the waist. They stood in each other's embrace.

"I just got an idea," Larry said. "When we move in, we'll have to christen all the rooms. We could get a head start on that right now." The sound of their laughter echoed throughout all the rooms.

Shae became Mrs. Lawrence Bethune Walker a month later. The wedding took place at the Holy Ghost Church of Jesus Christ Purchased by His Blood. Vivian insisted upon paying for everything since she had missed six years of her younger sister's life. Vivian and Richard had spared no expense. The church was decorated so beautifully that it was breathtaking.

Shae wore a flowing, white gown with a long train trailing behind. She looked radiant as she walked down the aisle to join Larry. Toby, standing tall and proud, gave his sister away. Vivian stood in as the matron of honor. Both sets of twins took part in the ceremony. Charles and Chris held the ring between them. Rasheda and Rameyra tossed rose petals out of a pail. They looked so cute in their identical dresses with frills. James even got the chance to attend the ceremony. He stood next to Larry as the best man. He looked handsome and mature decked out in his Army uniform.

That day was the happiest day of Shae's life. The time that she'd been a project queen was easily forgotten. She now was a true queen, Larry's queen, and that was all that mattered.

EPILOGUE

He had followed the case on Court TV. Today, he watched anxiously as the jury filed back into the courtroom to make a decision. When they ruled in favor of sentencing Bertha to a mental facility for fifteen years, his heart sank. Tears formed in his eyes.

He had failed her. That woman whose unemotional face appeared in a close-up as the camera zoomed in was his wife. Not only had he failed her, he'd deserted his family. And that's how they'd ended up.

He'd left them in those rat-infested projects, and he hadn't looked back. The *St. Petersburg Times* had a special section in the *Weekender* that held the entire story of the Byrts family. There would be a three-part series. He held the first part in his hands.

Behind These Walls of Pain: the Exposé of a Woman Gone Mad

St. Petersburg, FL – Bertha Byrts was ordered to serve the next fifteen years of her life in a mental facility. A jury of her peers convicted her. She's accused of poisoning her own mother and six-year-old, twin sons. The two children have made a full recovery. Mrs. Mary C. Mitchell, affectionately known as Ma Violet didn't fare so well.

What could have gone so wrong in this woman's life? What could push someone over the edge to the extent of taking out a $100,000 insurance policy on each family member? Read the riveting story in this week's special series, *Behind These Walls of Pain: the Exposé of a Woman Gone Mad.*

Jimmy couldn't see the words on the paper through his blurred vision. Posted on the pages that followed were pictures of his wife and children. Something burned deep within his chest. He'd left them behind to live in poverty. His wife had struggled to raise those five children alone. He hadn't even bothered to send one dime in child support.

But if any provide not for his own, and specially for those of his own house, he hath denied the faith, and is worse than an infidel.

That verse from the Bible came to him and he sank to his knees, begging God for forgiveness. He cried and prayed for a long time. Eventually, he felt calmness, a sort of inner peace, and he got up from the floor. Somehow, he'd make it up to his children. Bertha was lost to him now, but he could still reach out to his sons and daughters. It was never too late to change.

THE END

Dear Reader,

I hope you enjoyed reading PROJECT QUEEN. If so, I would appreciate it if you would help others enjoy this book too.

Review it. Tell other readers why you liked this book by reviewing it on Amazon, Barnes & Noble, Kobo, Smashwords or whichever website from which you purchased it.

Recommend it. Help other readers find this book by recommending it to your Facebook friends, Twitter followers, readers' groups and discussions boards.

Lend it. The eBook version of this book is lending enabled, so please, share it with a friend.

e-Gift it. eBooks make perfect gifts for avid readers!

P.S. I love to hear from my readers. Please connect with me online.

Novels

1. Big Tobe: Retribution
2. Ex-boyfriend
3. Fetish
4. Food Stamp Bitches
5. Headlines
6. In Need of a Joshua Man
7. Panzina's Passion
8. Project Queen
9. Project Queen 2
10. Real Hood Wives of St. Pete., The
11. Spin Cycle
12. They Call Me Mr. G-Spot
13. Uncrossing Her Legs
14. Unpretty Secrets
15. What About Your Friends
16. When There Are No Tomorrows

Novellas

17. My Cousin, Lenore
18. Under the Oak Tree
19. Unseen Wounds

Young Adult Titles

20. Janell Has an Attitude
21. Sequoia Denise, Just a Kid

Short Stories

22. Boy Who Needed Someone & Other Stories, The
23. Christmas Morning

24. Daddy Never Loved Me
25. How Many Licks
26. Office Grapevine
27. Power in Words, The
28. She Gets What She Wants

<u>Boxed Sets</u>
29. Hot Urban Fiction Mix 1
30. Hot Urban Fiction Mix 2
31. Hot Urban Fiction Mix 3
32. Project Queen Collection
33. Project Queen/Big Tobe Collection
34. Whatever Teen Series Collection

ABOUT THE AUTHOR

Teresa D. Patterson is the author of several novels, novellas and short stories. She is the founder of Edit Again Publications and has a degree in business.

To find out more information about the author, for book orders, and/or to read book excerpts, please visit her website: teresadpatterson.net

You may also join her on Facebook, Twitter and Blogspot.

CONNECT WITH THE AUTHOR

Twitter:
https:/twitter.com/teresapatterson

Facebook:
www.facebook.com/teresadiannapatterson

Blogspot:
http://teresadpatterson.blogspot.com

Pinterest:
http://pinterest.com/TeeRee1

Email:
teresadpatterson2004@yahoo.com

Made in the USA
Lexington, KY
03 December 2017